BY THE EDITORS OF
CONSUMER GUIDE™

MEDICAL BOOK OF REMEDIES:

50 Ways to Lose

TEN POUNDS

In Association With
DUKE UNIVERSITY DIET & FITNESS CENTER

JOAN HORBIAK, R.D., M.P.H.

PUBLICATIONS INTERNATIONAL, LTD.

Author: Joan Horbiak, R.D., M.P.H.
Consulting Organization: Duke University Diet &
Fitness Center
Editorial Assistance: Claire Boasi, Ed.D., M.S., R.D.
Coordinating Consultant: Dawn Schiffhauer, R.D.,
M.B.A.
Consultants: Ronette L. Kolotkin, Ph.D.
Peggy Norwood Keating, M.A.
Illustrations: Lane Gregory; Terry Presnall
Cover Illustration: Leonid Mysakov

The Duke University Diet & Fitness Center was founded in 1969 to help people live healthier, fuller lives through weight loss and lifestyle change. The Center's professional staff includes physicians, clinical psychologists, exercise physiologists, registered dietitians, and massage therapists. The team helps clients plan strategies and form new, healthier habits for life.

Joan Horbiak is a registered dietitian and president of Health and Nutrition Network, where she has designed and implemented programs for weight reduction and worksite nutrition. She has most recently served as a media and resource spokesperson for the American Dietetic Association (ADA) and is active on many advisory panels including ADA nationwide workshops on nutrition techniques for a low-fat lifestyle.

Claire Boasi is a health professional who has worked in the areas of weight loss and nutrition and has taught nutrition at the University of Pennsylvania and Drexel University. A registered dietitian, she has served on the board of directors of the American Dietetic Association and the Society for Nutrition Education.

Dawn Schiffhauer is the administrative director of Duke University Diet & Fitness Center. Her past experience includes developing a medically supervised weight-control program affiliated with St. Luke's-Roosevelt Hospital and a position as director of food and nutrition service at Mercy Catholic Medical Center.

Ronette L. Kolotkin is the director of the Behavior Program at Duke University Diet & Fitness Center, providing individual and group therapy. She has conducted research in obesity and binge eating and is a member of the American Psychological Association.

Peggy Norwood Keating is the fitness director for Duke University Diet & Fitness Center, where she develops and implements patient-education programs in fitness and exercise activities. She has certification as a fitness instructor from the American Council on Exercise and is a member of the American College of Sports Medicine.

C O N T E N T S

INTRODUCTION

How many times have you lost ten pounds, only to gain it back again? If this sounds familiar, you're not alone.

Lasting weight control doesn't come easy. The problem is, many people try to change too much, too fast. They go "on" a diet, which means that they'll go "off" at some point.

The program in this book is not a diet. Rather, it's a compilation of the top 50 nutrition, behavior, and exercise strategies for losing weight and optimizing health and fitness. Based on the latest research, the remedies provide you with specific strategies to achieve your goals.

The big difference here is that you make choices and changes that are right for you, but gradually so that they actually become part of your lifestyle. These choices and changes can help you lose 5 pounds or 20 pounds as well as they can help you lose 10; and they can help you keep the weight off.

What's the best way to start? It depends on you. Not all the remedies will apply to you, so congratulate yourself on what you're already doing right. But look to see where there is room to improve.

Tips For Getting Started:
1. Begin by choosing the sections of the book and the remedies that fit your interests and needs. For example, if eating a home-cooked meal is a rare event, see the remedies in "Slimming Ways to Dine Out." If you're finding food labels hard to decipher, see the remedies in "Shopping Smart in the Supermart."

2. Practice one or two remedies from a section for a few weeks until you reach your "comfort zone." It takes at least three weeks for a new behavior to become a habit.

3. When you're ready, move on to the next remedy. Just think of this book as your full-time coach.

As you try the remedies in this book, you'll see that lasting change can be achieved. Remember, small changes, taken one at a time, can add up to a lifetime of feeling good, looking good, and being the best you can be. But, the first step is up to you. Start now!

1

PUT YOUR WEIGHT-LOSS IQ TO THE TEST.

Are your thoughts and habits keeping you fat? Believe it or not, the biggest obstacle to losing weight can be your own misconceptions about dieting. Take this quiz to see just where you stand. If you agree with the statement, circle the number. Then read the answer to arm yourself with the latest facts, so that you'll know what works and what doesn't.

1. If I skip breakfast or lunch, I will lose weight faster.
Eating fewer meals can actually lead to weight gain and added body fat. In fact, one study showed that people who skip breakfast have a four to five percent lower metabolic rate (the rate at which your body burns calories to maintain vital functions when at rest) than those who do not. When you skip meals, your body fights back by slowing down the rate at which you burn calories. Believe it or not, you will lose weight more efficiently if you eat several mini-meals a day rather than one or two large meals. (See remedy 9 for more on this.)

2. I've heard that a calorie is a calorie, so it doesn't matter whether I splurge on 600 extra calories from prime rib or from pasta.
All calories are not created equal. Studies show that calories from fat are more fattening than those from carbohydrates. The body stores fat easily, but its ability to store carbohydrates is limited. That's why you'll gain more weight from eating an extra 600 calories of a fatty food such as prime rib than of a carbohydrate-rich dish such as pasta. Remember that the composition of your diet can be more important than the number of calories you consume. See remedy 8 for simple steps to zap fat.

3. I want to lose weight, but unless I lose it fast, I know I won't stick with the program.
If you lose weight fast, you are more likely to lose some muscle. Think of muscle as your body's engine. The larger the engine, the more gas it burns. If you lose too much muscle during weight loss, your engine becomes smaller and you need less "gas," or fewer calories, to keep it running. As a result, you'll actually gain weight if you eat the same number of calories that you previously consumed to maintain your old

> **FYI**
>
> Studies show that calories that come from dietary fat are more fattening than are calories that come from carbohydrates in the diet.

weight. Losing weight fast makes it harder for you to keep the weight off in the long run.

4. *I know that I can't eat at my favorite restaurants and still lose weight.*

It's possible to go into any kind of restaurant today—from fast food to five star—and still lose weight. Granted, you may have less control over how the foods are prepared and which ingredients are used, but you can control which foods you choose and how much of them you consume. The secret is to know how to approach the restaurant challenge. See the remedies in "Slimming Ways to Dine Out" to discover how to read between the menu lines and order foods so that they're prepared "your way."

5. *I must vow never to eat "real desserts" again in order to reach my goal weight.*

You don't have to give up your favorite foods or "goodies" to lose weight. Most people eat for pleasure as well as nutrition. If you love pie á la mode, just eat it less often and/or in smaller portions. Better yet, think substitution, not elimination. See remedy 13 to uncover ways to satisfy your sweet tooth without gaining weight, and see remedy 6 to develop an eye for portion size.

6. *I know the best way to lose my flabby stomach and thighs is to do sit-ups and leg lifts.*

Sorry—spot reducing just doesn't work. When you lose fat, it comes from your total fat reserves, and you have no control over what part of the body those fat reserves will come from. Spot exercises can tone and strengthen specific areas. But, aerobic exercise—such as brisk walking, jogging, cycling, or aerobic dance, for example—is the best way to burn fat. The bottom line: You'll burn more fat from around your middle (as well as from other fat-laden areas) if you take a brisk 20-minute walk than if you do 100 sit-ups. See the remedies in "Getting Physical."

7. *I would rather jump in the sauna and sweat off a few pounds than exercise.*

You can't bake, sweat, or steam pounds off. Sweating without exertion causes only a temporary water loss, not a fat loss. The water lost will be quickly regained as soon as you have anything to eat or drink. And remember, sauna suits, rubber belts, and nylon clothes designed to make you sweat during exercise can actually damage your health. It's important to replace fluids lost during exercise and allow your body's natural thermostat to regulate your temperature.

8. I will only feel successful if I reach my target weight.
Success means more than a number on the scale. It is an ongoing process that is rewarded each time you make a positive lifestyle change. So, don't be a slave to your bathroom scale. Put your time and effort into what really counts: keeping accurate records, using the remedies in this book, and increasing your daily activity. Habits, not pounds, will determine whether or not you achieve long-term success.

9. If I can't exercise strenuously, it really won't help me lose weight.
All activity counts. In fact, the American College of Sports Medicine recommends that adults exercise at a moderate intensity for at least 30 minutes a day, a few days a week. What's great about this recommendation is that these 30 minutes can include:

- Exercise in several shorter periods throughout the day.

- More-moderate activities, such as gardening and housework, as well as planned vigorous activity, such as jogging and cycling. See the remedies in "Getting Physical" to learn more.

10. I just don't have the willpower it takes to lose weight and keep it off for good.
Lasting weight control is a process that takes "skillpower," not willpower. By identifying your eating habits, using the remedies in this book, and thinking positively, you can tackle your weight and win.

2

SIZE UP YOUR BODY IMAGE BEFORE YOU SLIM DOWN.

Close your eyes and picture yourself as you look today—from head to toe. Pay particular attention to the size and shape of your body. That picture, what we sometimes refer to as our "body image," has a powerful influence over our weight-control efforts.

Look at the figures below, and put a check mark above the one that looks most like you now. Then answer the questions that follow.

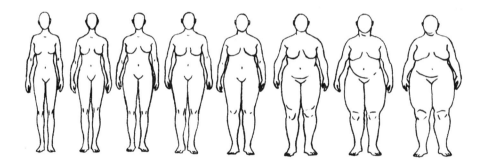

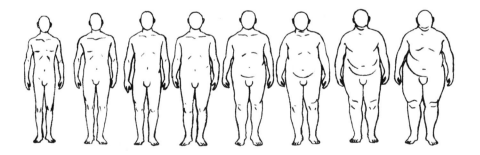

- If your best friend were to be totally honest with you, would they concur with the image you've checked?

- Which body image would you most like to look like? Circle it.

- What would your body weight be if you looked like the image you've circled?

- Have you ever been at this weight before?

Sometimes, you may perceive your body as appearing much heavier than others perceive it. Many women experience this phenomenon. If so, it's possible that you may continue to see yourself as heavy even after losing weight. You may also have difficulty noticing changes and giving yourself credit for the progress you've made.

On the other hand, you may still hold your high-school yearbook picture in your mind as your current body shape. If a realistic assessment moves you several silhouettes larger, you may not realize how much excess weight you have to lose. Procrastination may delay you from beginning your weight-loss efforts.

It's very important to begin any weight-loss process with a realistic body image. To promote change, you must clearly visualize yourself becoming more and more like the silhouette you've circled. Get in touch with your body as you embark on your weight-loss journey with these few simple tips for helping you make the mind-body connection:

Mirrors: Spend time looking in full-length or three-way mirrors, preferably without clothes on. Be fully aware of how your body currently looks, and congratulate yourself on all progress at it occurs.

Clothing: Alter large or loose-fitting clothes to stay connected to your body. Try clothes that are more form-fitting to help you adjust to your changing image. Don't save your "fat clothes"—it's like making a commitment to fail. Save one item of larger clothing to remind you of your progress.

Photographs: Take several photographs of yourself every four to eight weeks. Create a photo journal of your progress toward your weight-loss goals.

3

QUIETLY CONSIDER YOUR QUALITY OF LIFE.

We often hear about the high cost of shedding excess weight. But how often do we consider the cost of not shedding those unwanted, extra pounds? As health-care reformists add up the billions of dollars it costs to treat diabetes, heart disease, and cancer, researchers at Duke University's Diet & Fitness Center have been calculating the toll overweight takes on our overall quality of life.

What price would you pay for increased self-confidence, an improved self-image, a better love life, improved relationships at work and home? **Before going on to the next remedy, answer the questions on the facing page and learn how much your weight currently impacts your quality of life.**

If you answered "sometimes true" or "always true" to more than four of these questions, your weight is having a negative impact on your quality of life. If you answered "sometimes true" or "always true" on ten or more of these questions, your quality of life may be diminished dramatically by your weight.

The good news is that even small reductions in excess body weight net big returns when it comes to improved quality of life.

Try this on yourself: For the next four weeks, follow the tips in this guide that target areas of your lifestyle and behavior that you'd most like to improve. Then come back to this survey and answer these questions again. Note how your responses have changed. Recognize and give yourself a pat on the back for those areas in which you've improved. Remember, not all of the benefits of a healthy lifestyle are measured by the number that pops up on your scale each week.

Because of my weight...	Always True	Sometimes True	Never True
I feel physically uncomfortable.			
I feel socially unacceptable.			
I am self-conscious in social situations.			
I am afraid of being rejected.			
I am less productive than I could be at work.			
I am afraid to go on job interviews.			
I feel clumsy and awkward.			
I avoid recreational or social activities that involve physical activity.			
I feel unsure of myself.			
I am very moody.			
I have difficulty being assertive.			
I don't like myself.			
I feel out of control.			
I spend a lot of time worrying about my weight.			
I do not feel sexually attractive.			
I have little or no sexual desire.			
I don't want anyone to see me undressed.			
I do not enjoy sexual activity.			
I have difficulty finding clothes to fit me.			
I avoid activities where wearing a bathing suit or shorts is expected.			

4

RATE YOUR READINESS FOR CHANGE.

Change can be exhilarating and exciting; it can also be frightening and stressful. As you consider making changes toward a new, healthier lifestyle, it's important to assess your attitude toward change. We'll define attitudes as "consciously held beliefs." Before beginning any process of change, it's particularly important to understand whether your attitudes will move you toward, or away from, the goals you set. To help assess your attitudes, honestly answer the following questions:

T   F   Losing enough weight to reach my goal weight would guarantee me everlasting happiness.

T   F   It's a good idea to save my larger-size clothes just in case I need them again.

T   F   I find myself hating people I see in exercise classes or jogging down the street.

T   F   When I'm exercising and eating right, I get angry and frustrated when the scale doesn't show immediate results.

T   F   I feel deprived when I'm dieting and can't wait until I'm off the diet so that I can have my favorite foods again.

T   F   Once I lose weight, I'll look so good that I won't have to exercise anymore.

T   F   It's not fair that other people eat more than I do and don't have a weight problem.

T   F   In order to stay at my goal weight, I need to deprive myself and miss out on life's fun.

T   F   Someday I'll be able to take a pill that will allow me to eat all I want and still lose weight.

T   F   I view exercise as torture or punishment.

T F   Unless I lose five pounds per week, I feel discouraged and want to go off my diet.

T F   It's impossible to have an active social life and still lose weight.

T F   Keeping a food diary is childish and embarrassing.

T F   Food is my best friend.

T F   I feel panicky if food is not available when I want it.

T F   It's impossible for me to lose weight because of my family history.

T F   Once I begin exercising, if I miss more than a day or two, I feel I've blown it, so I quit.

T F   It's impossible for me to deal with life's stresses without turning to food.

> ## HINT
> Before beginning the process of weight loss, it's important to assess whether your attitudes will help move you toward, or away from, your goals.

If you answered "true" to more than four of these questions, you have some attitudes that may not move you toward your goals. It's important to identify and change these attitudes in order to lose weight permanently. If you answered "true" to ten or more of these questions, failure to change these destructive attitudes is likely to result in your being unsuccessful at keeping weight off once you've lost it. You may want to seek the assistance of a support group or of a mental-health professional.

5

HARNESS THE POWER OF THE PYRAMID.

The Food Guide Pyramid is a new way to visualize the foods you eat each day. It's a guide that helps you choose a diet that's right for you. Eating the "Pyramid way" gives your body the nutrients it needs while keeping your fat intake low. You simply count servings of food rather than calories.

Here are some specific tips to help you trim down while using the Pyramid:

- Pick the number of servings from the lower end of the range mentioned for each food group.

Food Guide Pyramid
A Guide to Daily Food Choices

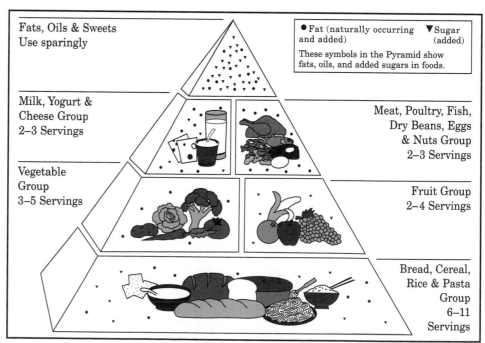

Note: Be sure to check the box on the next page to see what counts as a serving in each food group.

- Zero in on the selections from each group that are lowest in fat by first reading the remedies in "Shopping Smart in the Supermart." The "Shopping Smart" section has all the best bets in the supermarket.

- Build your diet from the bottom up. The location of food groups on the Pyramid corresponds with the number of recommended servings you should eat daily. For example, you should try to eat the most servings from the group at the Pyramid base—bread, cereal, rice, and pasta—and the fewest from the Pyramid tip—fats, oils, and sweets.

- Remember, no one food group is more important than another. Each food group provides some, but not all, of the nutrients that your body needs.

- The number of daily servings in some of the food groups may seem overwhelming at first. But if you look at the "What Counts as a Serving?" box below, you may find that you usually eat more than one serving of some foods, such as bread, at one meal. With a little planning, you'll soon discover that following the Pyramid is a simple way to meet your nutrient needs.

WHAT COUNTS AS A SERVING?

Bread, Cereal, Rice & Pasta (Grains) Group
1 slice bread
1 oz. ready-to-eat cereal (see package for cup equivalent)
½ cup cooked cereal, rice, or pasta

Fruit Group
1 medium piece of raw fruit (an apple, banana, orange, peach, or plum, for example)
½ cup cut-up raw fruit
½ cup canned fruit
¾ cup fruit juice

Vegetable Group
1 cup raw, leafy vegetables
½ cup cut-up raw vegetables
½ cup cooked vegetables
¾ cup vegetable juice

Meat, Poultry, Fish, Dry Beans, Eggs & Nuts Group
2-3 oz. cooked, lean meat, poultry, or fish

May substitute for 1 oz. meat:
½ cup cooked dry beans
1 egg
2 tbsp. peanut butter

Milk, Yogurt & Cheese Group
1 cup milk or yogurt
1½ oz. natural cheese
2 oz. processed cheese

Fats, Oils & Sweets Group
Use sparingly

6

DEVELOP AN EYE FOR PORTION SIZE.

Portion sizes can make or break your weight-loss plan. For example, you may start your day with a bran muffin and some whole-grain cereal. Sounds like a dieter's dream. But your bran muffin is bigger than a football and has more fat than a chocolate-covered doughnut. To make matters worse, your "industrial-sized" cereal bowl weighs in at about five servings, or 500 calories, according to the label!

MEASURING FOOD AT HOME

Use measuring cups to measure liquids, cereals, vegetables, pasta, and salad.

Use a food scale to weigh foods.

Use measuring spoons to measure jelly, sugar, peanut butter, margarine, salad dressing, and mayonnaise.

Be honest. When in doubt about your portion size, overestimate its size, and if necessary, reduce the amount.

The number of calories you eat depends not only on what you eat but also how much you eat. Even lean food choices can be a dieter's downfall if portions are oversized. Keeping tabs on how much you eat is the key to managing your calories and your weight.

Many people underestimate how much they're really eating. That's why it's critical to keep measuring utensils handy. A food scale for weighing portions and a set of measuring cups and spoons are a good investment. The chart on the next page is a useful tool, too.

Start out by measuring and weighing the foods you eat most frequently. Read food labels or see remedy 5 to find out how much of a food is in a standard serving. For example, the standard three-ounce serving of lean steak contains about nine grams of fat. But if you always eat a seven-ounce steak, you're getting 21 grams of fat!

If you find that your helpings are not always standard serving sizes, gradually cut back. For example, if you normally have three slices of bacon, try two. Also, try to serve your foods in standard portion sizes by dividing larger portions into two or more servings on your plate to develop a sense for standard portions.

This may all seem tedious at first. But once you become familiar with what a serving looks like, you'll be able to judge food on sight. Then you'll be able to go to a party or restaurant and guess the weight of a portion of food with a minimum of effort. Eventually, you will only have to weigh or measure foods from time to time to spot check for accuracy.

YOUR GUIDE TO PORTION SIZES

Meat, fish, and poultry

3 oz. cooked =
- a piece the size of a deck of cards
- amount in a quarter-pound burger (cooked)
- 4 oz. of boneless, raw meat
- 3 meatballs, each the size of a golf ball
- ½ large chicken breast
- ½ of a cornish game hen
- 2 chicken legs
- an 8"×2½" fish fillet, ¼" thick

1 oz. cooked =
- a piece of meat the size of a matchbox
- ¼ cup of chopped, cooked meat
- 2 cubic inches raw meat
- 2"×4" raw meat, ¼" thick
- a meatball the size of a golf ball

Restaurant and cafeteria portions:

1 serving of meat, fish, or poultry = typically 6 to 8 oz.
1 scoop of potatoes, vegetables, or cottage cheese = ½ cup
1 small scoop of ice cream = ¼ cup
1" cheese cube = 1 oz.
1 sandwich or hamburger cheese slice = 1 oz.
1 small ladle of salad dressing = 2 tbsp.
1 large ladle of salad dressing = 4 tbsp.
1 pat of margarine/butter = 1 tsp. of margarine/butter
1 heaping tbsp. of sour cream = 3 tbsp.
1 packet of creamer = 1 tbsp., or ½ oz.
1 small glass of wine = 4 oz.
1 can of beer or soda = 12 oz.

MEASUREMENTS TO KNOW

3 teaspoons (tsp.) = 1 tablespoon (tbsp.)

1 cup = 8 fluid ounces (fl. oz.)

2 tablespoons = 1 ounce (oz.)

1 cup = 16 tablespoons

4 tablespoons = ¼ cup

4 cups = 1 quart

1 pound = 16 ounces

7

SERVE IT RIGHT TO KEEP PORTIONS LITE.

Even when you know the right amount of food to eat, habits or even simply the sight and smell of food can keep you coming back for more. Now that you have a clearer picture of portion sizes, it's time to tackle some portion-control strategies. When serving foods, try to:

- Eat from dishes, not containers or bags. Eating ice cream from a half-gallon carton is a lot different than eating it from a cup. So, put everything on dishes, even if it's just a few crackers, cookies, or chips. This will help you break the habit of eating portions based on the size of the container rather than on true hunger.

- Do not keep serving dishes, bowls, or platters on the table during meals. If the food is right there, it's easy to take a few bites more. The key is to portion out your foods before bringing them to the table. If this isn't possible, put serving dishes at the other end of the table.

- Use smaller plates, bowls, and glasses to make your portions look larger. For example, put your food on a salad plate instead of a dinner plate. Serve beverages in a juice glass instead of a regular glass. Eat cereal from a cup rather than a bowl. One study showed that 70 percent of the people in a weight-reduction program were more satisfied with less food when it was served on a salad plate than when it was served on a dinner plate.

- Give away or store your "industrial-sized" dishes and mugs. They only lead to double-decker portion sizes. Remember that many times, we fill our plates out of habit, not hunger.

- Don't dive into the high-fat foods or entree first. Serve fiber-rich, high-bulk foods at the beginning of the meal. For example, try a hearty salad, fresh fruit, or lots of raw, crunchy vegetables for starters. This may help you feel satisfied with far fewer calories and minimize that starved feeling so you have better control for the rest of the meal.

- Serve food in standard serving sizes listed on food labels. For example, pour only one ounce of cereal. Get familiar with how much cereal is in one ounce. This will also help you judge portion sizes when you eat out.

- Don't bite off more than you can chew. In other words, take small bites of food, and chew thoroughly. Swallow what is in your mouth before preparing the next bite. Use a dessert fork instead of a dinner fork and a teaspoon instead of a tablespoon.

- Set some food aside. With each meal or snack, leave at least a couple of peas, a spoonful of rice, or a piece of bread on the plate. This can help you beat the "clean plate" habit. If you feel guilty, feed the scraps to the birds.

- Get rid of leftovers immediately. Many dieters eat more calories after the meal is over. For example, a person may eat a breast of chicken at dinner and then nibble on a bucket of chicken after dinner. The best way to prevent nibbling is to pack up leftovers quickly or turn on the disposal. What doesn't go to waste goes to your waist.

8

ZAP THE FAT IN MINUTES FLAT.

How can you squeeze the fat—and the calories that come with it—out of your diet? To find out, let's go on a fat-finding expedition to discover how to cut the fat, rather than the amount of food, for lasting weight control. The key is to take small steps, not quantum leaps. Lasting changes are most successfully made one small step at a time. For starters, try buying low-fat foods; bake, broil, poach, or steam them rather than frying; and season them with herbs and spices rather than covering them in cheese or creamy sauces. In addition, try some of the following substitutions.

INSTEAD OF:	TRY THIS:	YOU SAVE: Calories	Fat (g)
whole milk, 8 oz.	skim milk, 8 oz.	60	8
ricotta cheese, whole milk, 1 cup	ricotta cheese, skim milk, 1 cup	88	12
T-Bone steak, untrimmed, 4 oz.	London Broil, trimmed, 4 oz.	236	30
chicken breast, fried with skin and batter, 4 oz.	chicken breast, roasted without skin, 4 oz.	107	11
tuna, canned in oil, 4 oz.	tuna, canned in water, 4 oz.	77	8
clams, breaded and fried, 4 oz.	clams, steamed or canned, 4 oz.	164	10
duck, roasted with skin, 4 oz.	turkey, roasted without skin, 4 oz.	205	28
bacon, fried, 1 oz.	Canadian bacon, 1 oz.	111	12
peanuts, 1 cup	plain popcorn, 1 cup	815	71
creamed chicken soup, 1 cup	chicken noodle soup, 1 cup	116	10

INSTEAD OF:	TRY THIS:	YOU SAVE:	
		Calories	Fat (g)
french fried potatoes, 4 oz.	baked potato, 4 oz.	183	16
bran muffin, 1 large	blueberry bagel, 1 bagel	273	1
premium ice cream, 1 cup	ice milk, 1 cup	323	29
cherry pie, 1 slice	fresh cherries, 20	252	14
apple pie, 1 slice	baked apple, 1 apple	242	14
pecan pie, 1 slice	pumpkin bread, 1 slice	407	26
mayonnaise, 1 cup	light mayonnaise, 1 cup	942	112
margarine, 1 oz.	diet margarine, 1 oz.	103	12
Italian salad dressing, 2 tbsp.	Italian salad dressing, low-calorie, 2 tbsp.	105	11
guacamole dip, 1 cup	salsa dip, 1 cup	343	33

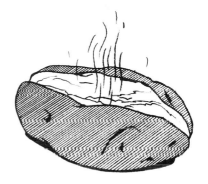

Now it's your turn. Think of at least three high-fat foods you eat frequently and low-fat foods you can replace them with. Write them here:

1. Instead of _____
   Try _____

2. Instead of _____
   Try _____

3. Instead of _____
   Try _____

Over the next week, try at least one of the low-fat substitutions you selected. Then make a new substitution each week.

9

GRAZE YOUR WAY THROUGH THE DAY.

Many dieters skip breakfast, skimp on lunch, and then gorge from dinner until bedtime. To put it simply, they cluster calories into one giant meal rather than spreading their food intake throughout the day. When the scale rises, they blame "nighttime eating" as the culprit. But that's not true.

The key issue is the spacing of meals, not the timing. It's harder to lose weight when you skip meals. When you starve yourself, your body retaliates by slowing down your metabolism (the rate at which you burn calories). Research has even shown that eating fewer meals can actually lead to weight gain, as well as reduced intakes of vitamins, minerals, and fiber.

Believe it or not, you will lose weight more efficiently if you eat several smaller meals a day rather than one or two larger ones. Spacing your food intake throughout the day will reduce the odds that you'll feel deprived or get so hungry that you end up overeating later on. It will also help to keep your blood-sugar and energy levels on an even keel.

Of course, that doesn't mean you can simply eat whatever you want all day long. You still must watch your calorie and fat intake. And indeed, some dieters experience a greater sense of control over food intake when they plan just three balanced meals per day. The point is that there's no benefit—and indeed there are likely to be negative effects—from trying to live on one meal a day.

Remember that you are the best judge of what meal plan will work for you. Here are some tips to keep in mind:

- Eat regularly. Don't go longer than five hours without food.

- Spread your caloric intake over four or five mini-meals eaten throughout the day instead of one large meal. You can break this down into three balanced meals and two healthy snacks if you find that such a plan helps to stave off hunger and gives you a better sense of control over your food and calorie intake.

- Keep mini-meals low in fat, because dietary fat more easily turns into body fat than either carbohydrate or protein does.

- Eat breakfast. It's important to provide your body with food throughout the day, during times when you are active.

- Plan snacks as a part of your day, especially at high-risk times such as mid-afternoon and mid-morning. See remedy 12 for your best snack bets.

- Include nutritious carbohydrates in your mini-meals. Use fruits, vegetables, beans, and whole grains to fuel your body and get a longer-lasting energy boost.

- Remember, skipping meals to cut back on calories only leaves you feeling tired, hungry, and deprived, making it harder to stick to your plan.

10

GET YOUR FILL FROM FIBER.

Everyone has heard about fiber. But how much do you really know? Circle the foods below that you think contain fiber.

beef jerky	pepperoni
kidney beans	string cheese
oranges	peanuts
green beans	chicken skin

Confused? This quiz proves an important point—texture is not a good indicator of a food's fiber content. The tough beef jerky, chewy pepperoni, stringy cheese, and rubbery chicken skin don't contain a speck of fiber. In fact, fiber is not found in any animal products.

Fiber is found only in plant foods, such as fruits, vegetables, whole grains, beans, nuts, and seeds. It's that part of a plant that our bodies cannot digest or break down. So, if you want to find fiber, first ask yourself, "Is this a plant or animal food?"

What does all this have to do with weight control? Plenty. There are five ways that fiber can help weight watchers:

• Many fiber-rich foods tend to be low in calories and fat and can replace or extend higher-fat foods.

• High-fiber foods bind water, giving your body a feeling of fullness and increased satisfaction. For example, it takes three large oranges to make a glass of juice. Would you feel fuller eating the oranges or drinking the juice? The juice is fiber-free while the oranges are fiber-packed.

• High-fiber foods slow down your eating pace because they take longer to chew. This gives your stomach a chance to signal your brain that you're full. And, since fiber is not broken down, it contributes practically no calories.

• High-fiber foods, such as whole grains, fruits, and vegetables, are packed with nutrients because they're less processed. Remember, when you cut calories, it's easy to rob your body of the nutrients it needs. So you need to choose nutrient-rich foods more often.

- Fiber has many other health benefits. Fiber comes in two forms: soluble and insoluble. Both perform valuable—but different—functions in your body, as shown in the accompanying chart.

THE DYNAMIC FIBER DUO

Insoluble Fiber	Soluble Fiber
• Does not dissolve in water	• Dissolves and forms a gel in water
• Tends to speed up food movement through the digestive tract	• Tends to slow food movement through the digestive tract
• Absorbs water, making stools softer and promoting regularity	• Does not promote regularity
• Helps prevent hemorrhoids and diverticulosis	• Helps lower blood-cholesterol levels
• May help prevent colon cancer	• Helps control blood-sugar levels in people with diabetes
Examples: wheat bran, whole grains	**Examples:** oat bran, beans, fruits, carrots

Note: Since soluble and insoluble fibers have different functions in the body, it's important to eat a variety of high-fiber foods in order to get both types.

Experts suggest that we aim for a daily target of between 20 and 35 grams of fiber a day. Unfortunately, the average American takes in only 11 to 13 grams of fiber per day—and some people eat considerably less. This means most of us should double our fiber intake.

Much to their digestive tracts' dismay, however, some people become fiber fanatics. They overload on fiber to reap the rewards faster. Keep these things in mind when adding fiber to your diet:

- Gradually increase the amount of fiber you eat. Your body needs to get adjusted to extra fiber. Adding fiber too quickly can cause gas, diarrhea, and bloating. So take it slowly.

- Drink plenty of liquids every day to keep fiber moving. Fiber helps prevent constipation by acting like a large sponge in the colon, holding water and keeping wastes moving. If there's not enough fluid available, fiber can actually block your digestive tract, resulting in constipation.

- Keep fiber intake to 20 to 35 grams a day. You can overdo a good thing. Fiber "keeps things moving" in your digestive tract, yet too much can cause an avalanche. In fact, excess fiber can decrease the amount of vitamins and minerals your body absorbs.

- Forget fiber pills. Many fiber pills contain only small amounts of fiber compared with the amounts found in food. For example, one brand has about half a gram of fiber in each pill. So, you would have to pop 50 to 70 pills a day to meet your fiber target. Besides, extracting fiber from foods and putting it in pill form may change the structure and effectiveness of the fiber.

There are some misconceptions about how to reach your daily fiber target. Many people think a salad a day will give them all the fiber they would need. In fact, you would need to eat 50 cups of iceberg lettuce to get your day's fiber requirement. And for those of you who think that "an apple a day" is enough, think again. The Food Guide Pyramid in remedy 5 recommends eating two to four servings of fruits, three to five servings of vegetables, and 6 to 11 servings of grains, breads, and cereals each day. By following these guidelines, you will be sure of getting ample amounts of fiber. The tips below can help you get the most fiber from your fruits, vegetables, and grains.

- Read the label. Foods that are a good source of fiber have three to five grams of fiber per serving. Foods that are high in fiber have five or more grams of fiber per serving.

- Eat foods in their most naturally occurring state. Processing, canning, and juicing tend to decrease the fiber in foods.

- Choose whole fruits instead of juice. Remember, some juices can provide lots of calories (a glass of carrot juice weighs in at about 220 calories) but zero fiber.

- Eat the edible peels and skins of produce such as potatoes and apples. Much of the fiber is found in this outer layer. And don't forget to eat some of the pith (the white membrane in oranges and grape-fruits).

- Include the stems when preparing vegetables such as broccoli.

- Eat fruits with edible seeds, such as strawberries and kiwis.

- Eat a variety of chickpeas, kidney beans, pinto beans, and black beans. Substitute them for part or all of the meat in recipes.

- Eat whole-grain breads and pasta, cornmeal, bulgur, brown rice, rye, and barley. Look for a bread with a whole-grain flour, such as "100% whole-wheat flour" or "stoneground whole-wheat flour," listed as the first ingredient on the label.

- Substitute whole-wheat flour for part of the white flour in your recipes for baked goods.

- Start your day with a whole-grain cereal that has three grams of fiber or more per serving.

- Fill your plate first with whole grains, fruits, and vegetables rather than using meat as the base or focus of your meals.

11

SLIM DOWN RECIPES TO ENJOY THE FOODS YOU LOVE.

Once you have stocked your kitchen with low-fat foods, you can exercise your culinary talents to slim down your meals. To cut fat and calories and/or increase the amount of fiber in your favorite recipes without sacrificing taste, try some of the easy-to-use substitutions listed here. Before long, you'll discover that small changes make a big fat difference.

When Your Recipe Calls For...	Use This...
1 whole egg	2 egg whites or ¼ cup egg substitute
1 egg yolk	1 egg white
whole milk	skim milk or skim-milk buttermilk
cream, half & half	evaporated skim milk
sour cream	nonfat or lite sour cream
mayonnaise	low-fat or fat-free mayonnaise
butter, margarine, oils (for greasing pans/sautéing)	nonstick pans and vegetable cooking sprays
butter, shortening, oils (for baking)	reduce the amount of fat by 25% and choose a preferred oil: canola, olive, safflower, or corn
regular cheese	fat-free or low-fat cheese with no more than 3 grams of fat per ounce
white sauce	use a mixture of 1 tbsp. margarine, 1 tbsp. cornstarch, and 1 cup evaporated skim milk
salad dressing	no-oil salad dressing

fat-based marinades	use ½ to 1 cup of flavored vinegar, orange juice, low-fat yogurt, defatted stock, wine, or fat-free salad dressing per pound of meat; *marinade examples:* chicken: use yogurt, dill, and garlic; beef: use red wine, vinegar, lemon juice, rosemary, thyme, and onions; fish: use orange juice, ginger, and garlic
white flour	use 50% whole-wheat and 50% white flour
white flour (for thickening only)	use 50% less cornstarch
white bread	whole-grain bread
sugar, honey	heat-stable sugar substitutes or reduce sugar by 25% and add nonfat milk powder, vanilla extract, and/or cinnamon
1 oz. baking chocolate	3 tbsp. cocoa and 1 tbsp. oil
pecans or nuts	dried fruits such as raisins or nugget-type cereal

12

OUTSMART YOUR SNACK ATTACKS.

Fewer and fewer consumers are sitting down to eat the traditional three squares a day. In a nationwide survey, only 50 percent of adults said they ate three regular meals a day. The term "grazing" was coined to describe the continuous snacking or frequent light-eating behavior of a growing portion of the population. Dashboard dining, grazing, and eating on the run are becoming norms for many Americans.

So, whether you're nibbling on carrot sticks or noshing on nachos, you're part of a growing trend. In fact, Americans eat over 19 pounds of snacks each year. This adds up to more than 42,000 calories for each person per year. Fortunately, more low-fat and fat-free snacks are appearing on the supermarket shelves. Still, the average amount of fat calories in snacks such as chips is 50 percent.

Here are some helpful strategies that you can use when the urge to snack strikes:

Exercise your options with the three-gram fat formula. Read the label and look for snacks that have three grams of fat or less for every 100 calories. This simple formula will help you choose snacks that get less than 30 percent of their calories from fat without having to do a lot of complex calculations. You'll be surprised at just how many different foods qualify as low-fat snacks.

Trade in the deluxe models for the new minis. If you haven't noticed, snacks are shrinking. Now you can buy everything from bagels to brownies in bite-size form. Minis deliver the great taste you love but take a smaller bite out of your daily calorie budget. For example, a bite-size bagel has just 70 calories, while the full-size version has about 150 calories. Crave a candy bar? Rather than spend 510 calories on the king-size Milky Way bar, savor the miniature for 110 calories. But say no to seconds.

Downsize your snacks. Simply turn large-size packages into safe solo portions by dividing and then rewrapping the contents in plastic bags. This is helpful, especially if a six- to ten-ounce bag of chips becomes your single serving. Another option is to go on "automatic portion control" by buying single-serve snack containers. Just remember to grab for just one serving when the urge to snack strikes.

Don't be fooled by "healthy snacks." Be careful with products such as banana chips, yogurt- or carob-covered candy, and mixed nuts or seeds. Many of these are still loaded with fat. For example, even though some banana chips are fried in "cholesterol-free" oil, they still get 60 percent of their calories from fat. And most nuts and seeds, even dry-roasted ones, are 75 percent fat or more. You could have 36 cups of plain popcorn for the same calories in one cup of nuts.

Keep portable snacks on hand. A snack attack can sneak up on you when you least expect it. Be prepared with these one-fisted snacks that are perfect for everything from dashboard to desktop dining:

- mini-bagels, rice or popcorn cakes
- low-fat crackers: graham, Rye Krisp, Wasa, Crispbread
- fresh fruit or small boxes of raisins
- single-serving cups of unsweetened applesauce, puddings, nonfat yogurt, or instant oatmeal
- snack-size boxes of cereal or pretzels
- pull-top cans of water-packed tuna, salmon, or soup

Fill up on fluids first. Many people confuse feelings of thirst for hunger. So enjoy a large glass of ice water, hot tea, low-sodium broth, or another calorie-free beverage before reaching for a snack. You may discover that you were really just thirsty.

Sit down, relax, and enjoy. A lot of people don't count what they eat while standing. Yet the results of this mindless nibbling become visible over time. For example, you may stand by the freezer and eat spoonfuls of ice cream throughout the day instead of portioning out a small bowl. What you don't realize is that those extra nibbles can add up to ten pounds of excess body fat in one year! Cut thousands of unconscious calories by making a rule to never snack while standing.

Don't go longer than five hours without eating. If you find that snacking is getting out of hand, take a closer look at your meals. When you skip meals or go more than five hours between meals, your body may cry out for snacks to get some of the calories that you should have gotten from your meals. A snack is meant to supplement, not take the place of, your meals.

Plan ahead. Anticipate your snack attacks and be prepared for them. If you get the mid-morning munchies or raid the refrigerator after work, build a snack into your morning or afternoon plan. Remember, a little extra planning—not willpower—is the key to preventing bigger binges later on. And stock your fridge with plenty of fresh fruits and raw vegetables so you can grab them quickly.

Get support from family members. Tell them to take charge of the snacks they eat and keep them in out-of-the-way places, such as a basement pantry or a cupboard you don't have to open every day. Or simply ask your family members to help you by not having your "problem" foods in the house. And don't rationalize that you are keeping your favorite ice cream or cookies around for your children when it's really for you! If you feel that you must keep calorie-laden snacks around, buy those that the family will eat but that are not appealing to you.

Don't deprive yourself! When you totally deprive yourself of the foods you love, you only increase their appeal. Then you usually wind up eating everything but the kitchen sink and remain unsatisfied until you get what you wanted in the first place. Why not try the low-fat versions of your favorite snacks? If visions of the "real thing" still dance in your head, satisfy your cravings with a small portion of the desired food. For example, if you get the urge for ice cream, go to the ice-cream shop and have a small cone.

As you can see, there's no need to give up those snacks that keep you going between meals. The key is to plan ahead and snack for the right reasons. In fact, if you eat smaller main meals, a healthy snack may actually help you lose weight faster (see remedy 9).

13

SATISFY YOUR SWEET TOOTH.

Your sweet tooth is probably more active than you think. Americans currently eat, on average, about 40 pounds of various sugars each year—that's 61,600 calories worth!

If that sounds hard to believe, take a look at the hidden sugars in some popular foods:

	Sugars (tsp.)
Low-fat fruited yogurt, 8 oz.	7
Fruit canned in heavy syrup, ½ cup	4
Chocolate bar, 1 oz.	3
Cola, 12 fl. oz.	9
Fruit drink, ade, 12 fl. oz.	12
Chocolate shake, 10 fl. oz.	9
Fruit pie, ⅙ of 8-inch pie	6

Sugar supplies calories and little else nutritionally. To make matters worse, oftentimes, sugar doesn't travel alone—its common companion is fat. For example, about 56 percent of the calories in fruit pies comes from fat; 53 percent of the calories in most chocolate bars comes from fat; and 65 percent of the calories in premium ice cream comes from fat. Does this mean you have to give up sweets? Absolutely not!

Fortunately, supermarkets are providing a wider variety of sugar-free foods than ever before. With the availability of thousands of good-tasting foods that use sugar substitutes, cutting sugar no longer means depriving yourself. Moreover, The American Dietetic Association released a comprehensive position paper in 1993 that supports the safety of sugar substitutes.

Here are some additional tips to satisfy your sweet tooth in the kitchen and at the store while trimming sugar and/or fat.

In The Kitchen:
- Every ½ cup of sugar adds nearly 400 empty calories. You can lower the sugar in some of your recipes by 25 percent and then add 25 percent more spice, such as cinnamon, nutmeg, or vanilla, to enhance the flavor. Cake recipes are more difficult, but you can

begin by cutting the sugar in these by only a tablespoon or two. Remember, you can't cut sugar completely; some sugar is needed for bulk, structure, and browning.

- Make pies with a single rather than a double crust, and you'll save about 100 calories per serving. Stick with crusts made of graham crackers, which are lower in fat and calories than flour-based crusts.

- Since much of the fat in cake is in the icing, use fruit purees or a light dusting of powdered sugar instead.

- To boost fiber, vitamins, and minerals, try substituting whole-wheat flour for all-purpose flour in many baked products. Start off with a 50 percent substitution.

  - Replace oil or other fat called for in cake, brownie, and muffin recipes or packaged mixes with an equal portion of applesauce or fruit purees. These natural fat substitutes can slash the fat by 75 to 90 percent. For example, one-third cup of applesauce, when substituted for oil in a store-bought yellow cake mix, will save 648 calories and 72 grams of fat.

  - In many recipes, you can use unsweetened cocoa powder instead of chocolate to cut the fat. Just use three tablespoons cocoa for each ounce of chocolate called for. Some recipes may need a teaspoon of oil added to keep the proper texture.

- Try evaporated skim milk instead of heavy cream to give your cheesecakes, sauces, puddings, and cream pies that creamy texture without loads of fat. You'll save 60 grams of fat per cup.

- Substitute two egg whites for each whole egg.

- Use nonstick pans and vegetable sprays when the recipe calls for a "greased" pan.

- Serve natural sweets. Bake or broil fruit for dessert. Try baked pears, bananas, or apples or a broiled peach. Enhance the flavor with cinnamon or nutmeg.

- If you get the urge to splurge on a rich and decadent dessert, try splitting it with a friend, and enjoy.

At The Store:

- You have to do more than look for the word sugar on the food label. Many products have sugar disguised under a variety of names. The names of some sugars that manufacturers add to foods are:

sucrose	lactose
glucose	mannitol
dextrose	honey
sorbitol	corn syrup
fructose	molasses
maltose	maple sugar

- Skip the honey. It is higher in calories than regular table sugar and contains no real nutritional value.

- If you eat cookies by the box and candy by the pound, don't keep them around the house. When you want a sweet that you tend to binge on, go to the store and buy one cookie or one candy bar, for example. That way you won't have seconds "on hand."

- Try some of the new lines of fat-free cakes and cookies. Watch serving sizes, however. These products may be fat-free, but they still have calories.

14

BELIEVE CLAIMS ON FOOD LABELS.

Weight-wise shopping has never been easier, thanks to the new nutrition label. Here's the good news: You can now believe the claims on the new food labels. In the past, terms such as "low-fat," "light," and "80% fat-free" were a minefield of misinformation because there weren't any standard definitions for them. For instance, a "light" snack could be higher in calories than the regular version because "light" referred to the food's texture—a "detail" that the manufacturer didn't tell you. Cheese wearing a low-fat banner could still be 75 percent fat. Even worse, a luncheon meat labeled 80 percent fat-free might contain a whopping 72 percent of calories from fat!

But misleading terms are history, and the path to health-wise shopping is less bumpy. Now, you can buy with confidence. Today, claims on product labels can only be used if a food meets new legal standards set by the government. So, if the cheese you're thinking of buying says "low fat," it really is a low-fat food. Rest assured, when you read the label, you will be able to get not only the truth, but the whole truth and nothing but the truth.

We can't explain all the new claims you'll be seeing, but here are the ones that every weight watcher should know:

LABEL LINGO

If the label says...	It means...
Calorie free	Less than 5 calories per serving
Low calorie	40 calories or less per serving
Reduced calorie	At least 25% fewer calories per serving when compared with a similar food
Light or Lite	⅓ fewer calories or 50% less fat; if more than half the calories are from fat, fat content must be reduced by 50% or more; non-nutritive "light" claims are allowed but must identify the basis of the claim (examples: "light in color," "light in texture")
Fat free	Less than ½ gram of fat per serving
Low fat	3 grams of fat or less per serving
Reduced fat or Less fat	At least 25% less saturated fat per serving when compared with a similar food
Lean	Less than 10 grams of fat, 4 grams of saturated fat, and 95 milligrams of cholesterol per serving
Extra lean	Less than 5 grams of fat, 2 grams of saturated fat, and 95 milligrams of cholesterol per serving

15

BREAKING DOWN THE FOOD LABEL.

The new food labels are finally here! Now most packaged food items in the grocery store are wearing up-to-date, easier-to-use labels. Not only do you get more information, but it's more accurate. So, get to know the new labels. They can be one of your best allies in helping you select a healthier diet to lose weight.

1. **Serving Size.** Serving sizes are now standardized and reflect the amounts most people actually eat. Getting a clear picture of your typical serving sizes, however, is essential to losing weight. Is your serving the same size as the one on the label—or do you eat the entire box?

Label tip: Face reality and multiply the calories and nutrients by the number of servings you really eat. Stick to the recommended serving size on the product label, and develop an eye for portion size by reading remedy 6.

2. **Calories from Fat.** Reducing fat intake is the single most important dietary step you can take to lose weight and reduce your risk of heart disease and cancer.

Label tip: To keep the total fat in your diet low, choose more foods with a big difference between the total number of calories and the number of calories from fat.

3. **List of nutrients.** This list covers those nutrients most important for your health.

Label tip: For fat, saturated fat, cholesterol, and sodium, choose foods with a low "% Daily Value." For total carbohydrate, dietary fiber, vitamins, and minerals, your daily value goal is to reach 100 percent of each nutrient.

4. **% Daily Value.** This is a new term that shows how a food fits into an overall daily diet of 2,000 calories. Here's how it works: If a food has 13 grams of fat per serving, the "% Daily Value" will be given as 20 percent, meaning it supplies a substantial amount (one-fifth) of the daily quota for fat. You can also use "% Daily Value" to compare products. If a serving of Brand A's cheese has a "% Daily Value" of 13 for total fat, compared to

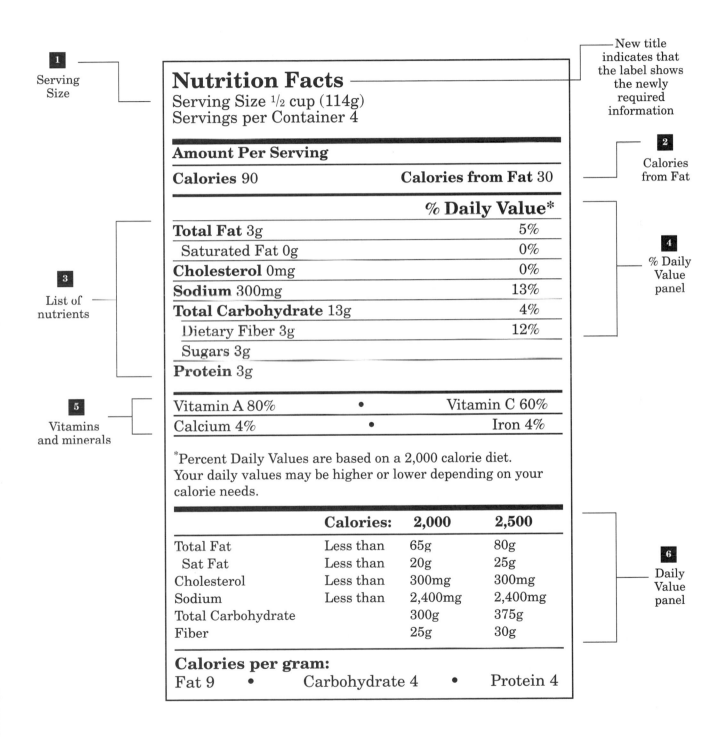

1
Serving Size

New title indicates that the label shows the newly required information

Nutrition Facts

Serving Size ½ cup (114g)
Servings per Container 4

Amount Per Serving

Calories 90   Calories from Fat 30

2
Calories from Fat

% **Daily Value***

Total Fat 3g	5%
Saturated Fat 0g	0%
Cholesterol 0mg	0%
Sodium 300mg	13%
Total Carbohydrate 13g	4%
Dietary Fiber 3g	12%
Sugars 3g	
Protein 3g	

4
% Daily Value panel

3
List of nutrients

Vitamin A 80%	•	Vitamin C 60%
Calcium 4%	•	Iron 4%

5
Vitamins and minerals

*Percent Daily Values are based on a 2,000 calorie diet. Your daily values may be higher or lower depending on your calorie needs.

	Calories:	2,000	2,500
Total Fat	Less than	65g	80g
Sat Fat	Less than	20g	25g
Cholesterol	Less than	300mg	300mg
Sodium	Less than	2,400mg	2,400mg
Total Carbohydrate		300g	375g
Fiber		25g	30g

Calories per gram:
Fat 9   •   Carbohydrate 4   •   Protein 4

6
Daily Value panel

Brand B's "% Daily Value" of 5, Brand B is the better choice for your weight-loss plan.

Label tip: Judge nutritional quality in a snap. If a food has 20 percent or more of the Daily Value, it's "high" in that nutrient. A food that contains 10 percent to 19 percent of the Daily Value is a good source of that nutrient.

5. **Vitamins and minerals.** Values for only two vitamins, A and C, and two minerals, calcium and iron, are required on the food label.

Label tip: Don't count on one "super food" to do it all. Your goal here is 100 percent of each vitamin for the day. Let a combination of foods add up to a winning vitamin score.

6. **Daily Value panel:** This panel gives you "the big picture" by showing you how much of each key nutrient you should have—or limit yourself to—each day based on a 2,000 or a 2,500 calorie diet. You must adjust these recommended values to your own calorie intake.

Confused? All these numbers can give anyone a bad case of indigestion. So, break the label into bite-size pieces. On your next supermarket trip, simply look at the top of the "Nutrition Facts" panel and focus on the Serving Size and Calories from Fat. After a few weeks, move to "% Daily Values." Before you know it, you'll be shopping smart.

16

ARM YOURSELF WITH THE TOP TEN SUPERMARKET SKILLS.

The supermarket is a minefield of marketing hype, advertising, and packaging. It is designed by experts who place food items in ways that make you buy more and buy impulsively. Have you ever wondered why all those candy bars are at the checkout stand or why many foods are packaged to look tastier than they are?

It's all planned to get to your food dollar—and it can end up getting to your waist. By arming yourself with some survival skills, you can bypass the colorfully packaged foods that offer little more than shelf appeal.

Here are the top ten supermarket survival strategies to control impulse buying. Write them down and carry them with you.

1. Plan ahead. Prepare a weekly menu, including regular meals and snacks. This will help you minimize impulse eating and the number of last-minute decisions about what to buy at the supermarket.

2. Make a list before you go shopping, and stick to it. Your list is a compass that will guide you on a safe course; without it, you may get hopelessly lost among the chips, dips, and corn curls. And by all means, make the list at home, after you have eaten.

3. Choose a nutrition-friendly grocery store. Look for shelf labeling, nutrition booklets, recipe cards, and a variety of healthy foods at reasonable prices. In fact, several chains now employ home economists and nutritionists to assist you in your selections.

4. Keep your shopping trips to a minimum—once a week, if possible. This saves time and saves you from temptation. And try to go alone or with a person who supports your weight-loss efforts.

5. Get into the label-reading habit. Check the serving size, calories, and fat per serving to be sure you know what you're getting. (See remedy 15.)

6. Bypass the danger zones—aisles filled with your "problem" foods and tasting islands with free food samples. The key is to leave your "problem" foods in the store, not at home where they can tempt you.

7. Shop when you aren't tired or hungry. Many studies have shown that the purchasing of high-calorie "junk food" soars when a shopper is hungry. If you eat before you go, you'll be less likely to buy impulse food items.

8. Do not overbuy or become coupon driven. Especially, avoid the economy size of "problem" foods. If you have trouble controlling your portion sizes, buy single-serve containers rather than half-gallon containers or buy snack-size packages of chips rather than the bushel bags. Then, you can eat the whole thing without blowing your plan.

9. Take your groceries home intact. Don't nibble on food in the store or on the way home. When you're waiting in the checkout line, check out the magazine rack instead of the candy rack. And put your groceries in the trunk or in the backseat, where you can't reach them during the trip home.

10. Ask your local grocery-store manager to stock any items you can't find. The wider variety of low-fat foods currently on your supermarket shelves is largely due to consumer requests.

17

SELECT THE SKINNIEST CUTS OF MEAT, FISH, AND POULTRY.

Shopping for meat can be a challenge, because most packages don't carry nutrition labels to help you make low-fat selections. The good news is that hogs and cattle have gone on a diet and are leaner than ever before. Now, if you watch your portion sizes and choose lean cuts, meat, poultry, and fish can fit easily into your diet. Look for the cuts listed here:

Beef
Round cuts: round tip,
top round, eye of round;
Loin cuts: top loin, sirloin, tenderloin

Ground meat
Ground round; 85 percent extra-lean;
Ground chicken or turkey breasts

Pork
Loin cuts: tenderloin, center loin chop;
Leg cuts: shank or sirloin portion; Boneless ham:
95 percent lean; Canadian bacon

Lamb
Loin chop and leg cuts

Veal
All types except the breast

Game Animals
Venison, Rabbit, Buffalo

Turkey/Chicken/Fish
All types except breaded or deep-fat fried

In addition, keep the following smart-shopper tips in mind when you visit the meat, fish, or poultry section:

• Buying lean cuts of meat and trimming the fat can pay big dividends. For example, the difference between a seven-ounce broiled round steak and a T-bone steak of the same size is 32 grams of fat.

The difference between a trimmed seven-ounce T-bone steak and an untrimmed one of the same size is 30 grams of fat.

- Use the "loin/round rule of thumb" for beef and the "loin/leg rule" for pork, lamb, and veal. Cuts with these words on the label will be lean choices.

- The standards for grading meat have nothing to do with nutritional value—they have a lot to do with fat. The grade that is lowest in fat is SELECT, followed by CHOICE, and then PRIME.

- Choose three-ounce servings (for a total of six ounces or less per day). Start with four ounces of raw meat to end up with a three-ounce cooked serving, which is about the size of a deck of cards.

- Buy skinless poultry, or remove the skin before eating. Peeling the skin off a half breast of roasted chicken reduces fat from about eight grams to about three grams and calories from 195 to 140.

- Dark meat of poultry contains about twice the amount of fat as the white meat does.

- Ground turkey or chicken usually is a mixture of white meat and dark meat, skin, and fat. Read the label, and be sure to buy ground turkey "breast" or ground chicken "breast." Better yet, ask the butcher to grind skinless breasts or cutlets, or grind it yourself.

  - When choosing whole turkeys, avoid butter-added or self-basting turkeys, which are injected with fats. Baste it yourself with sherry, cranberry juice, apple juice, or skimmed chicken or turkey broth. Cook poultry breast-side down to keep it nice and juicy without added fat.

- Dark-colored fish, such as salmon and swordfish, have more fat than whitefish. But they're filled with heart-smart fats called omega-3 fatty acids, so you can enjoy without guilt.

- Look for the following signs of freshness in fish:
  - Shiny, taut, and bright skin. Dull, brown, or dry gills spell "old."
  - Bright, clear, and bulging eyes. Sunken, milky eyes mean extended storage.
  - A clean, pleasant smell. Bypass fish that smells fishy.
  - Firm flesh that springs back when pressed with your finger. If a dent remains, the fish is past its prime.

18

CUT THE FAT, NOT THE CALCIUM, AT THE DAIRY COUNTER.

Whether you're six or sixty, you never outgrow your need for calcium. Calcium not only builds strong bones and teeth, it will also help to maintain strong bones in adults. Especially for women, getting enough dairy foods in the diet is vital, since these foods are the best sources of calcium. Unfortunately, dairy products are also packed with fat and calories. However, keeping the calcium while cutting the fat is easy if you try the countless varieties of low-fat dairy products. On your next trip down the dairy aisle, look for these choices:

Milk: skim, 1% and 2%, nonfat powdered milk
Evaporated skim milk
Buttermilk: skim and low-fat
Yogurt: nonfat or low-fat
Cottage cheese: dry curd, nonfat, 1%, and 2%
Cheese: nonfat or low-fat
Sour Cream: nonfat or low-fat
Egg substitutes

In addition, keep the following smart-shopper tips in mind when you visit the dairy section:

- Most whole-milk cheeses get 70 to 80 percent of their calories from fat, which is more than some meats. Even some of the lower-fat cheeses are 60 percent fat. Buy cheeses with less than three grams of fat per ounce. At home, control portions by grating or shredding cheese instead of eating slabs or slices.

- Don't be fooled by cream cheese—90 percent of its calories come from fat. Even the "light" cream cheeses get about 75 percent of their calories from fat. And many people pile on more cream cheese than they do butter. Use "light" ricotta cheese instead of cream cheese as a spread, or try fat-free cream cheese.

- Gradually shift from drinking whole milk to skim milk. Whole milk has about two pats of butter in each cup, two-percent milk has about one pat, and skim has practically none. The calories you would save in a year by drinking two cups of skim milk each day instead of two cups of whole milk are equivalent to ten pounds.

- The calcium content of low-fat dairy products is equal to full-fat dairy products, so you won't be losing out on this bone-building nutrient.

- Buy dairy products in paper or opaque packaging. Florescent light used to illuminate display cases in grocery stores can actually rob vitamins from your dairy products.

- Evaporated skim milk makes a great fat-free coffee creamer. Chances are, you won't be able to tell the difference. Remember: Half-and-half gets 78 percent of its calories from fat while many nondairy coffee lighteners get 90 percent. Stay away from nondairy powdered creamers that are made with saturated palm or coconut oil.

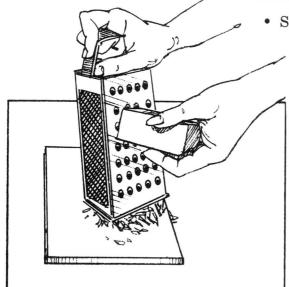

- Skip the yolks. An egg white has no cholesterol and only 16 calories, while the yolk has 213 milligrams of cholesterol and 60 calories. Use two egg whites or an egg substitute for each whole egg in recipes or omelets.

- Some fruit-flavored yogurts have up to eight teaspoons of added sugar. Add your own fresh fruit to plain or vanilla yogurt to boost fiber.

- Regular sour cream has about one-fifth the calories of butter or margarine. And now you can try the new fat-free varieties for even greater savings.

19

TAKE FIVE AND THRIVE.

Leading health experts agree that eating five servings of fruits and vegetables a day is one of the most important choices you can make to maintain health and lose weight. Unfortunately, only about ten percent of Americans eat this much daily.

Don't be part of these grim statistics. Fill up your shopping cart with vibrant tastes, textures, and flavors from a variety of fruits and vegetables. They're naturally low in calories and fat.

While all fruits and vegetables are good for you, be sure to include those that are high in vitamin A (dark green and deep yellow in color) and vitamin C every day. You should also eat vegetables from the cabbage family (cruciferous vegetables) several times a week.

Rich in Vitamin A

carrots	broccoli	spinach
sweet potatoes	cantaloupe	peaches
tomatoes	apricots	

Rich in Vitamin C

grapefruits	oranges	strawberries
kiwi fruit	cantaloupe	papaya
citrus juices	peppers	cauliflower
broccoli	cabbage	potatoes

Cabbage-Family Vegetables

broccoli	cauliflower	cabbage
	brussels sprouts	

Whichever way you slice it, fruits and vegetables are a must on everyone's shopping list. To help get you started—and to help you get the most out of fruits and vegetables—here are some tips:

- Don't drink all of your fruit. Fresh fruit gives you the satisfaction of chewing, takes longer to eat, and helps you feel fuller because it's filled with fiber. Plus, it's lower in calories than juice. One cup of grapes, for example, has 60 calories, while one cup of grape juice has 155.

- Practice portion control with dried fruits. Dried fruit can contain as much as 70 percent sugar by weight, or more than many cookies. As a result, calories can add up quickly. For example, a cup of raisins weighs in at 450 calories, while a cup of grapes has only 60 calories.

- If you drink juice, make sure it's 100 percent juice. Go easy on fruit drinks, punches, and "ades," which contain very little juice and more sugar than a regular soda. Twelve ounces of fruit drink, ade, or punch has about 12 teaspoons of sugar and 185 calories; 12 ounces of soda has only 9 teaspoons of sugar and 160 calories.

- To stretch calories, use water or club soda to dilute higher-calorie fruit juices such as cranberry or grape.

- Forget the great grapefruit hoax. Many diets claim that grapefruit contains an enzyme that burns fat. To set the record straight, there are no known enzymes that will increase the rate at which fat burns. Granted, grapefruit is low in calories, but there's nothing in it that will make the pounds disappear.

- An avocado weighs in at about 300 calories and has 30 grams of fat. Although the type of fat is heart healthy, it still has as many calories as any other type of fat. So, trade in your guacamole for salsa, and save 340 calories per cup.

- Select fresh or frozen vegetables without sauces. Sauces add lots of sodium as well as fat. For example, one cup of frozen cooked broccoli, with no fat or salt added during cooking, weighs in at 50 calories, 0 grams of fat, and 40 milligrams of sodium. One cup of frozen broccoli with cheese sauce, on the other hand, tips the scales at 180 calories, 11 grams of fat, and 780 milligrams of sodium.

- Remember, potatoes are filling, not fattening. It's how they're topped that counts. Use salsas, mustards, low-fat cottage cheese, or fat-free sour cream as potato toppers.

20

EAT MORE CARBOHYDRATES TO WEIGH LESS.

Limit calories! Cut fat! What's left to eat? The answer is complex carbohydrates—breads, cereals, whole grains, pasta, and other starchy foods. The latest word on these superstars is to make them a staple of the diet. Experts agree that we should get 6 to 11 servings from this group.

With starchy foods, you can eat more and weigh less. Here's why:

- They're low in fat and calories.

- They don't turn into body fat as efficiently as high-fat foods.

- They can be used to stretch high-fat foods.

- They help fill you up by providing fiber and bulk.

Swapping carbohydrates (or "starchy" food) for fatty foods can also boost your energy levels, giving you the fuel you need to achieve peak performance throughout the day. Here are some wise carbohydrate choices to include in your meal plan:

Breads
100% whole wheat
Stone ground, multigrain, cracked wheat, oat, or rye
English muffins, bagels
Pita bread
Hard rolls, buns
Corn tortillas

Cereals
All bran cereals
Flakes or puffed cereals: whole-grain wheat, rice, or oats
Oatmeal, oat bran, whole-grain hot cereals

Grains, Rice & Pastas
All types

Beans & Tofu
All types

In addition, keep the following tips in mind when shopping for carbohydrates:

- For a fiber boost, buy breads and cereals that list "whole wheat" or "whole grain" as the first ingredient. Don't be fooled by words like "wheat flour" or "enriched wheat flour," which are nutritionally equivalent to white flour.

- Choose breads and cereals that have less than two grams of fat per serving. Also, look for cereals that have at least four grams of fiber and less than eight grams of sugar per serving.

- Compare serving sizes of cereals. Although one ounce is the standard, many people eat more than that. For example:
  1 oz. of a puffed cereal = 1 cup
  1 oz. of flakes = ¾ cup
  1 oz. of a dense cereal like granola = ¼ cup

- When preparing packaged foods, don't slavishly follow all of the directions on the label. Experiment with using less fat and salt and perhaps adding herbs and spices instead. Add only half the fat called for, omit the salt, and use skim milk instead of whole milk. By trimming the fat, you can buy convenience foods such as macaroni and cheese, seasoned rice and pasta mixes, scalloped potatoes, and stuffing without guilt. If you need to watch your sodium intake, read those labels carefully, however. Some convenience foods are loaded with sodium.

- Bypass high-fat biscuits, croissants, muffins, scones, and doughnuts. Be especially aware that some baked goods may *sound* healthier than they actually are; some bran muffins, for example, have more calories than chocolate-covered doughnuts. Reach for bagels and English muffins instead.

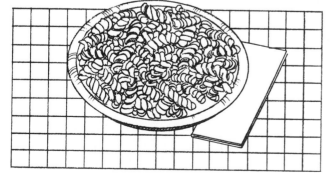

- Be adventurous. Experiment with barley, bulgur, couscous, and buckwheat groats as a change of pace from rice or potatoes. If you have trouble finding any of these, ask your grocer to stock it, or check a health-food store.

- Keep several types of pastas handy to make a great meal in minutes. But don't oversauce your pasta. The sauce should complement pasta's distinctive flavor, not mask it.

- Tofu, or bean curd, is a powerhouse of protein. It's also wonderfully low in calories (about 20 calories per ounce), while the leanest beef or chicken provides about 50 calories an ounce.

- Go meatless once or twice a week. Use dried beans and peas in place of meat, fish, or poultry in your meals. Beans are also good in salads, soups, sandwiches, sauces, and, for a different kind of "snack," as a bean dip.

- Switch proportions. Make sure that the pasta, rice, potatoes, and grains take up more room on your plate than the meat, poultry, or fish does.

21

DE-GREASE YOUR SHOPPING CART TO DECREASE YOUR CALORIE INTAKE.

Getting the excess fat out of your diet is the fastest way to cut those extra calories. Fat packs over twice the number of calories (250 per ounce) that pure protein and carbohydrate have (115 calories per ounce). Studies also show calories from fat count more because they are more readily stored as body fat.

While fat is essential, the average person eats six to eight tablespoons, or about a stick of butter per day. However, your body requires only one tablespoon a day. Here are some wise choices to help you squeeze the fat out of your supermarket cart:

Nonstick vegetable sprays
Butter-flavored granules
Margarines: reduced calorie or diet
Salad dressings and mayonnaise: fat-free or reduced calorie
Vinegars: white, red wine, flavored, balsamic

In addition, here are some tips to keep in mind when selecting fats and oils:

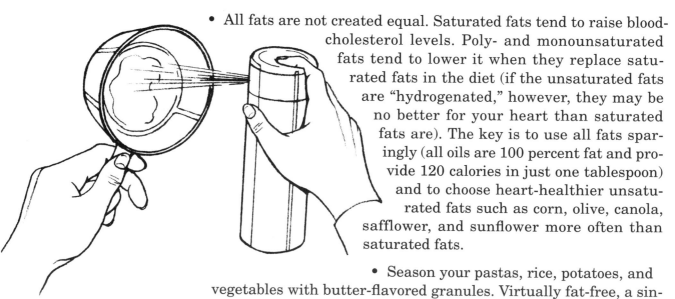

• All fats are not created equal. Saturated fats tend to raise blood-cholesterol levels. Poly- and monounsaturated fats tend to lower it when they replace saturated fats in the diet (if the unsaturated fats are "hydrogenated," however, they may be no better for your heart than saturated fats are). The key is to use all fats sparingly (all oils are 100 percent fat and provide 120 calories in just one tablespoon) and to choose heart-healthier unsaturated fats such as corn, olive, canola, safflower, and sunflower more often than saturated fats.

• Season your pastas, rice, potatoes, and vegetables with butter-flavored granules. Virtually fat-free, a single teaspoon is only eight calories and replaces the 108 calories and 12 grams of fat found in a tablespoon of butter.

- Margarine has about the same number of calories as butter. To cut calories, try apple butter, jelly or jam, or a little cinnamon to add flavor to your toast.

- If you use a nonstick vegetable spray once a day in place of one tablespoon of butter or margarine, you'll save about ten grams of fat and 92 calories. Make this switch each day for a year, and that's almost eight pounds of fat you won't use.

- Try the new reduced-fat or fat-free versions of foods you eat regularly. Reduced-fat margarine, salad dressings, and sandwich spreads can expand your food choices while curbing your fat tooth.

- Read the ingredient list. Margarine with water listed as the first ingredient has ⅓ to ½ less fat than the average margarine. But don't cook with these, since their high water content makes them splatter.

- Choose liquid or tub margarines over stick margarines. The softer a fat is at room temperature, the less saturated it is and the better it is for your heart.

- Be aware that "light" or "lite" oils may only be light in color and flavor, not in fat. And "cholesterol free" does not mean fat-free.

- If you can't lick the butter habit, use whipped butter rather than stick. Not only is it lower in calories, it spreads more easily, so you may use less.

22

STOCK UP ON CANNED STAPLES FOR CONVENIENCE THAT COUNTS.

Canned foods are hard to beat for convenience. However, from a nutritional standpoint, fresh is best, frozen runs a close second, and canned comes in last. Canned foods are zapped with heat that can destroy some of the C and B vitamins. Minerals can also be lost if the canning liquid is discarded. And finally, large amounts of sodium are often poured in during processing.

Clearly, the canned-food aisle is a challenge. To help you get started, here are some acceptable choices:

Tuna, salmon, and fish: water-packed
Soups: broth, tomato-based, and bean
Beans: peas and lentils
Fruit: packed in juice or water
Juice: unsalted tomato and vegetable juices
Vegetables: lower-sodium varieties of vegetables, water chestnuts

In addition, here are some tips to help you choose and use canned foods wisely:

- When using canned foods, drain them, then rinse them at least one minute. This can cut the salt by about 40 percent.

- To cut fat, read the label. Pick canned foods with no more than three grams of fat per 100 calories.

- Calories add up fast when sugar or syrup is used in canned fruit. For example, a half cup of fresh unsweetened peaches has only 36 calories, while a half cup of peaches canned in heavy syrup has 95 calories.

- Watch out for nuts and seeds. Just a handful may contain 16 to 20 grams of fat, equal to the amount in four to five teaspoons of margarine. And don't be fooled by the dry-roasted nuts; they get 74 percent of their calories from fat.

- To add lots of crunch without lots of calories, add water chestnuts rather than nuts to meals and salads.

- Salted tomato juices contain 600 to 750 milligrams of sodium per cup. Give the new "lite" and lower-sodium varieties a try; they contain only 40 to 50 milligrams.

- Use your "bean" and stock up on cans of chickpeas, kidney beans, pinto beans, and black beans. Beans are power packed with protein, fiber, vitamins, and minerals. If beans cause flatulence problems, you can help to turn off the gas by first draining and rinsing canned beans; this will reduce gas-forming sugars as well as extra sodium. Then, cook the beans thoroughly to make their starch easier to digest. In addition, and especially if you are new to bean cuisine, begin with smaller portions and increase your intake gradually. Finally, if these tricks don't work, you might try a few drops of an over-the-counter product called Beano. It contains a natural enzyme that helps to break down the sugars that lead to gas.

- If soup is your choice, choose broth or tomato-based soups, which are lower in fat than creamed types.

Soup (1 cup)	Calories	Fat (g)	Sodium (mg)
chicken broth	25	0	895
chicken broth, low sodium	25	0	49
Manhattan clam chowder	70	2	800
New England clam chowder	165	7	1002

- Whether you're using canned or homemade soup, refrigerate it overnight so that the fat rises to the top and hardens. Then you can simply lift off the fat before you heat the soup. If you don't have time, throw a few ice cubes in the soup, which will make the fat rise.

- Prepare canned soups with water or skim milk rather than whole milk. Or opt for some of the new lower-fat and lower-sodium soups.

- Skip the oil. Use low-sodium chicken broth for sautéing, stir frying, flavoring rice and pasta, and pan simmering fish and poultry.

- Choose canned fish packed in water rather than oil. If you use oil packed, drain and rinse it first to cut the fat and sodium.

Tuna (3.5 oz.)	Calories	Fat (g)
oil-packed	300	20
drained, oil-packed	200	8
drained, water-packed	131	0.5

- Keep in mind that sardines and salmon canned with soft, edible bones are also packed with calcium. No bones, no calcium.

- Buy the individually packaged containers of applesauce and fruit. They're the perfect snack for a quick and nutritious bite when you're on the run.

23

BLAZE A LOW-CALORIE CONDIMENT TRAIL.

The condiment aisle is overflowing with products that can add flair, flavor, and pizazz to your meals. When choosing condiments, however, it's vital to keep tabs on the calories, fat, and sodium. These little extras can really add up fast.

For example, a tablespoon may not seem like much over the course of a day or when it's added to a sandwich. But depending on what's in the spoonful and how often you eat it, you could be in trouble. If you used an extra tablespoon of mayonnaise every day for a year, you could find yourself carrying around ten extra pounds of body fat.

So, go easy on the extras, and measure them with care when you do use them. Below is a list of calorie-containing condiments—some are bargains, some aren't.

CONDIMENTS COUNT!

Condiment (1 tbsp.)	Calories	Sodium (mg)	Fat (g)
apple butter	37	0	0
barbecue sauce	12	127	0
butter	108	123	12
catsup	16	156	0
chili sauce	17	191	0
chutney, mango	41	4	0
horseradish	6	14	0
jam, jelly	49	14	0
mayonnaise	100	80	11
mustard	12	188	0
pickle relish	21	107	0
soy sauce	11	1029	0
steak sauce	18	149	0
sweet & sour sauce	32	320	0
tartar sauce	75	220	8

24

ROUND OUT DIET FROZEN MEALS WITH POWER FOODS.

Too busy to cook? You're not alone. The days of *Leave It to Beaver* families, where mom's at home cooking all day, are over. In fact, studies show that most cooks want to spend less than 30 minutes in the kitchen preparing a meal, and 20 percent of cooks spend less than 15 minutes actually doing so. So what's a busy dieter to do?

There are many ways to balance convenience and nutrition in the frozen-foods section of your grocery. You may even burn some calories in your search because the average new supermarket has 700 linear feet—more than the length of two football fields—of frozen products.

The good news for weight-conscious folks is that the number of healthful frozen dinners and entrees is growing. You can now find hundreds of meals-in-minutes that are low in fat, calories, and sodium. Even health professionals who once gave frozen foods the cold shoulder are now giving their seal of approval to some of them.

But how can you take advantage of the convenience that frozen meals offer and still be assured that you're getting the nutrients you need for good health? It's easy. By reading the labels carefully and adding some power foods to round out the meal, you can thaw, unwrap, and "zap" a nutrient-packed meal. Here are two important steps to get you started:

STEP 1:
Read the label to make sure the meal you're buying is a frozen asset. The meal you choose should supply no more than 300 calories, no more than ten grams of fat, and less than 800 milligrams of sodium per serving.

STEP 2:
Round out frozen meals with healthful additions, such as a whole-grain roll and fresh green salad. The following is a listing of the top ten foods to give your frozen meals the winning nutritional edge. Rounding out frozen meals will also help fill you up so you'll be less tempted to reach for seconds.

1. Low-fat/nonfat milk and yogurt
Key nutrients: calcium, protein, riboflavin
Pointers: Try to add one serving of low-fat milk or yogurt routinely to your frozen meals. Or for a scrumptious dessert shake, blend one cup of your favorite fruit with half a cup of the milk or yogurt, some ice, and water. Remember, low-fat milk and yogurt are two of the richest sources of calcium, which can help keep bones healthy and ward off osteoporosis.

2. Broccoli
Key nutrients: vitamins A and C, calcium, fiber
Pointers: Broccoli is the king of vegetables and the ideal side dish for frozen meals. One stalk (cooked) offers 100 percent of your daily requirement for vitamin C. Also, bones love broccoli because it is one of the few calcium-containing vegetables; one cup provides 140 milligrams of calcium.

Steaming and microwaving preserve most of the nutrients. Don't smother broccoli's benefits with a high-fat cheese sauce. For a satisfying yet low-fat topping, try freshly squeezed lemon juice, a sprinkling of parmesan cheese, or a sharp herb such as fresh thyme.

3. Spinach/leafy greens
Key nutrients: vitamins A and C, folic acid, iron, fiber
Pointers: Salads and frozen meals are perfect partners for fast nutrition. But if you still rely on pale iceberg lettuce, now is the time to go for the greens. The deeper the color, the higher the nutritive value. For an even greater change of pace, microwave or stir fry your greens in a teaspoon of olive oil, and season with fresh herbs.

4. Whole-grain breads, rolls
Key nutrients: B vitamins, fiber, complex carbohydrates
Pointers: To boost fiber, round out your meals with a crusty whole-grain roll, bread, or crackers. At the market, check the label and select breads and rolls that list "whole wheat" or "whole grain" as the first ingredient.

5. Red and green sweet peppers
Key nutrients: vitamins A and C, folacin, fiber
Pointers: Peppers are loaded with vital nutrients, especially vitamin C. By weight, green bell peppers have twice as much vitamin C as cit-

rus fruits (red peppers have three times as much and are a good source of vitamin A).

Chopped sweet peppers can enhance your salads and cooked vegetables. You can also try stir frying them in a small amount of olive oil or low-sodium broth. Use thin strips to garnish and boost the nutrients of any of your frozen meals. For a tasty treat, broil peppers five minutes on each side and cool in a brown paper bag.

6. Cantaloupe
Key nutrients: vitamins A and C, potassium
Pointers: Fruits high in vitamins A and C are ideal side dishes for frozen meals. Half a cantaloupe will meet your daily requirement for both vitamins A and C as well as provide valuable minerals such as folacin and potassium. A cup of cubed cantaloupe has more potassium than a banana.

Serve cantaloupe plain or chilled with a squeeze of lime juice, or slice and toss it with fresh berries. For an extra-special treat, top it with low-fat frozen or regular yogurt and a dash of cinnamon or nutmeg. On a hot day, puree cantaloupe for a refreshing sorbet.

7. Tomatoes
Key nutrients: vitamins A and C, potassium
Pointers: Tomatoes are a perfect no-work addition to frozen meals. One medium tomato has only about 35 calories and supplies 40 percent of your daily requirement for vitamin C and 20 percent of the requirement for vitamin A. Layer fresh tomato slices on a plate with fresh basil leaves, or create a salad of chopped red and yellow tomatoes. For a tasty treat, halve tomatoes; sprinkle them with herbs, breadcrumbs, and a little grated cheese; and broil for five minutes. Try not to refrigerate your tomatoes, however. Cold kills their flavor.

8. Carrots
Key nutrients: vitamin A, potassium, fiber
Pointers: Carrots are the number one dietary source of vitamin A; a 3½ ounce serving of raw carrots provides over 500 percent of your daily requirement. Toss cooked carrots with a squeeze of lemon juice or add

a little honey and orange juice to coat with a light glaze. Or combine carrot sticks with wedges of tomato as part of a vegetable platter.

9. Strawberries
Key nutrients: vitamin C, potassium, folacin, fiber
Pointers: Low in calories and packed with vitamin C, a serving of eight medium strawberries provides hearty amounts of potassium and folacin and a good supply of fiber. Try them plain, toss them into a fruit or lettuce salad, or whirl them in a blender with nonfat yogurt and a splash of juice for a frothy drink.

10. Brussels sprouts
Key nutrients: vitamins A and C, folic acid, potassium, iron, protein
Pointers: Low in calories and a leading source of vitamins A and C, brussels sprouts are also a good source of vegetable protein, with 31 percent of their calories coming from protein. Toss cooked sprouts with lemon juice and nutmeg, toasted sesame seeds, water chestnuts, or strong seasonings such as dillweed, sage, and garlic. You can also sauté steamed sprouts in a teaspoon of olive oil with fresh garlic.

25

STOP THE VITAMIN ROBBERS.

When you cut calories, it's easy to rob your body of the nutrients it needs. So it's important to get the biggest nutritional bang for your buck by eating more fruits and vegetables.

There's just one catch. There are vitamin robbers that can sabotage your produce and your best intentions. Here are some easy ways to protect your fruits and vegetables from the top four vitamin robbers: time, chopping/peeling, heat, and water.

Time
- Vitamins degrade after four to five days. So, shop when your grocery receives its produce shipment.

- Don't buy more food than you can use. Fresh produce stored indefinitely in your refrigerator loses vitamins. If you want vegetables but may not use them quickly, buy frozen vegetables.

- Cook only the amount of vegetables you can eat, and serve them promptly. The longer food stands, the higher the nutrient losses. Leftover vegetables, for example, can lose up to 50 percent of their vitamin C after two to three days.

Chopping/Peeling
- Don't peel produce. The outer skin, the leaves, and the area just below the skin have more vitamins, minerals, and fiber than the center.

- Avoid buying precut vegetables, since vitamins are lost when the surface is exposed to air.

- Keep vegetables whole until you are ready to cook them. Minimize chopping and trimming.

Heat
- Select fresh or frozen over canned vegetables when feasible. Canned vegetables are exposed to a heating process that can destroy some of the C and B vitamins.

- Cook vegetables until they are barely crisp-tender, not limp or mushy. Overcooking destroys vitamins.

Water

- Some vitamins dissolve in the water used to cook, soak, or wash fruits and vegetables. So wash produce just before serving, and avoid soaking.

- Scrub surfaces with a vegetable brush.

- Try to cook vegetables and fruits with the skins on. Even if you don't eat the skin, leaving it on during cooking helps protect the vitamins.

- Cook above, not in, water as much as possible. Use a steamer or the microwave.

- If you must boil vegetables, use the least amount of water. Vegetables covered with water sometimes lose as much as 100 percent of their vitamin C; use an amount of water equal to half the volume of the vegetable or less. Bring water to a boil, add vegetables, and cover with a tight-fitting lid to decrease cooking time. The remaining liquid is a storehouse of nutrients; use it to make soups, sauces, and stews.

- If you cut produce, limit the surface area that is exposed to the cooking water by chopping it into large chunks rather than dicing or finely chopping it.

26

ASK FOR IT YOUR WAY WHEN DINING OUT.

With the average American eating one-third of their meals away from home, there are lots of opportunities for overeating. But you don't have to choose between losing weight and dining out. You can have both if you learn some new skills to use before, during, and after the meal to insure that your calorie and fat intake stays on track. In fact, many restaurants are changing their menus to suit weight-conscious customers.

The take-charge techniques below can help you expand your restaurant choices without expanding your waistline.

TODAY'S SPECIALS

Broiled lemon sole — Steamed vegetable medley

BEFORE THE MEAL...

Bank calories. Banking calories is easier than balancing your checkbook—and a lot more fun. Simply save calories (by eating less) earlier in the day or week, so you can afford to eat more when you go out. Keep in mind, though, that banking calories means cutting back on calories—not skipping meals—prior to eating out.

Move that body. Burn some extra calories by increasing your physical activity for a few days before or after dining out.

Decide on your general order before you go to a restaurant. If you wait until you get there, you're a goner. Tantalizing descriptions of the food can sabotage your best intentions. For example, broiled fish sounds just plain dull next to the fettucini Alfredo or eggplant parmigiana. One option you can use in a restaurant that you visit frequently is to never open the menu. You can ask for the fresh fish of the day, a baked potato, and a salad and be set calorically and nutritionally.

Beat the starve-stuff cycle. A lot of people skip meals throughout the day so they can stuff themselves at the restaurant. Once locked into this cycle, they lose control and eat more calories in one restaurant meal than they would have in three. Granted, it's a good idea to bank calories, but skipping meals is risky. The key is to never go to a restaurant hungry. To curb your appetite, eat lighter meals and then a small snack, such as a bagel, crackers, fruit, or yogurt, an hour before you go. And make your dinner reservations for earlier in the evening so that you won't be famished when you do eat.

Pick a place that fits your plan. Call the restaurant in advance and ask about the menu. Also, ask if special requests are honored. Pass up places made for gorging, such as those with all-you-can-eat specials, buffets, and dessert bars. Also, don't hesitate to review the menu before you take a seat.

Order first. Did you ever notice how people follow suit when ordering? The power of suggestion can easily change your mind. For example, you may want coffee for dessert, but after hearing your friends order chocolate cheesecake and mud pie, you talk yourself into the double-fudge nut brownie. Sound familiar? By ordering first, you will be less likely to change your mind, and others may follow your lead.

Ask questions. Remember that you are the customer—don't be afraid to ask for what you want. For example, ask how menu selections are prepared and what ingredients are used. Are the meats, chicken, or fish broiled with butter or other fat or served with sauces? Are vegetables buttered or creamed?

In addition, ask servers what they would suggest as a light entree. They can often create a lean dish that's not listed on the menu. Inquire, too, about the availability of food items not listed on the menu, such as low-fat or skim milk and fresh fruit.

Speak up. Use "could you" to make these slimming requests and save thousands of calories:

For appetizers, could you...
...remove the bread, butter, chips, fried noodles (or other complementary table tempters you don't want) from the table?

...serve the appetizer as my main course with the other entrees?

...serve the salad dressing on the side with some vinegar and lemon wedges?

For the main course, could you...
...use fish or chicken in place of the beef in this dish?

...use more vegetables and less meat in this dish?

...prepare this dish with less or no added fat or butter?

...serve the sauce on the side?

...remove the chips, cheese, mayonnaise, bacon, nuts, (or other fatty accessories you can't afford) from my dish?

...replace the fries with a baked potato or vegetable?

...replace the croissant with whole-wheat bread?

...wrap the leftovers in a doggie bag? (Caution: If you dive into that doggie bag later that night, leave it at the restaurant or give it to a friend next time.)

For dessert, could you...
...bring extra plates and spoons so we can split this order?

DURING THE MEAL...

Fill up on volume first. Start your meals with water, diet drinks, salads, and clear soups rather than buttered rolls and rich appetizers. This will "dampen" your appetite before the main entree arrives.

Eat slowly. You've probably paid top dollar for your meal, so why not savor the flavor of every bite? Besides, it takes 20 minutes for your brain to tell your stomach you've had enough to eat. So chew every mouthful at least five to eight times. See remedy 37 for more tips on slowing down at mealtime.

Be choosy. Eat what you enjoy the most first, and leave the mediocre food behind.

Never, ever clean your plate. Restaurant portions are usually too large, and if you order a full-course meal, the volume of food can be overwhelming. For example, dinner portions of meat are usually eight ounces, and most restaurants serve two chicken breasts. Ask if "petite" servings or half-portions are available. Other options to trim down the amount you eat include choosing an appetizer as your main dish, ordering á la carte, sharing with a friend, and asking for a doggie bag. And remember, rarely does the last spoonful taste as good as the first one or two.

Go easy on alcohol. Alcohol adds calories fast and can make your weight skyrocket. See remedy 31 for ways to drink and be merry without blowing your diet.

Think thin thoughts. Your thoughts can work for or against you. Here are a few tips to overcome the most fattening restaurant thoughts:

"I've paid for it, and I want to get my money's worth."
If this is your mind-set, by all means, avoid all-you-can-eat places and price-fixed meals in which every course is included. Keep in mind, when dining out, you pay for more than the food. So, try to look beyond the food. Restaurants also offer a relaxed atmosphere, a change of scenery, and an excuse to avoid cooking and dirty dishes. Try to enjoy the company, the conversation, and the luxury of being waited on more than you enjoy the food on your plate.

"It's a special occasion. It won't hurt to have it just this once."
People who buy into the "just this once" mentality are on a dieting roller coaster. Their weight goes up and down based on their social calendar. If it isn't dinner out, it's a party, a wedding, or Thanksgiving dinner. Try considering every day as the same—that is, in terms of your eating habits.

"I've had a hard day, I deserve this."
Reward yourself instead with a movie, sports tickets, or some other activity you enjoy. Or simply take an hour off to do exactly what you want to do instead of what you have to do.

AFTER THE MEAL...
Have the table cleared of leftovers immediately.
Or make remaining food less visible by covering it with your napkin. Remember, out of sight means out of mind.

Skip dessert, or share one. If you really decide to splurge, get some extra spoons, take a bite, and pass your dessert around the table. It probably won't make it back to you.

Avoid the post-meal slump. How many times have you felt like taking a nap after eating out? Drowsiness hits, especially after large meals, because the heart pumps extra blood and oxygen to your digestive tract and away from your brain. To offset this post-meal slump, end your meal with a short walk or a little stretching.

27

SURVIVE THE FAST-FOOD JUNGLE BY ORDERING WISELY.

These days, fewer people are sitting down to three square meals a day. Instead, dashboard dining, eating on the run, and fast foods are becoming a way of life for many of us. Fortunately, now you can have low-fat food to go!

Many fast-food chains have gone on a health kick and now offer items such as low-fat shakes, no-fat muffins, "lite" chicken, and whole-grain cereals. Of course, the triple burgers are still around.

So, you can enjoy fast foods if you're choosey. Before you order, ask for nutrition brochures. Many fast-food chains have published calorie, fat, and sodium information for their menu items. The values can vary significantly from item to item and chain to chain.

Here are some quick tips to help you choose weight-wise fast foods.

The Main Course:
• Avoid items that sound bigger than life—"double deckers" or "super," "jumbo," or "extra large" anything. For example, there's a difference of roughly 300 to 600 calories between the small and super burgers. Even if you eat two small burgers, the calorie total can be less than one of the deluxe models. Better yet, order roast beef for a leaner option than most burgers.

	Calories	Fat (g)
Hamburger	260	9
Roast Beef	260	9
McLean Deluxe	320	10
Quarter Pounder	410	20
Big Mac	500	26
Big Classic	570	33
Whopper with cheese	706	44
Double Whopper with Cheese	935	61

- All chicken sandwiches are not created equal. Some of them can actually be higher in fat than a cheeseburger. The secret is to pick the right chain and order the right sandwich. For a change of pace, take your taste buds south of the border and try a low-fat chicken fajita.

	Calories	Fat (g)
Wendy's Grilled Chicken Sandwich	290	7
Burger King Broiler Chicken Sandwich	379	18
McDonald's McChicken Sandwich	415	19
McDonald's Chicken McNuggets	270	15
McDonald's Chicken Fajita	185	8
McDonald's Chicken Breast Sandwich	250	4

- "Have it your way" by asking them to hold the secret sauces, mayonnaise, and tartar sauce. One dollop can add 150 to 200 calories of pure fat. Pile on crisp lettuce, fresh tomatoes, and onions instead. Even the catsup and mustard are better bets since they have virtually no fat.

- When you crave fried chicken, skip the "extra crispy." Extra crispy means extra fat—there can be as much as a hundred calories more per piece. Strip all or some of the greasy breading and skin off. And do yourself a favor—choose the chicken breast, not the entire bucket.

- Pizza is one of your best bets, as long as you order vegetable toppings. Pass on the extra cheese, olives, and meat toppings. To really slim down, try a "no cheese" or "half the cheese" pizza with extra tomato sauce and veggies. It sounds spartan, but it's really delicious. Stick with the thin crust rather than the pan and deep-dish crusts, which are loaded with hidden fats.

- Check out the chili. It's packed with protein, fiber, vitamins, and minerals, yet it's usually relatively low in fat and calories. The small chili at Wendy's, for example, has 190 calories and six grams of fat.

- Many fast foods are sodium traps. To make matters worse, it isn't always easy to predict which foods have the most sodium. A milk shake, for example, has more sodium than the fries. To balance fast foods, especially if you are sodium sensitive, skip canned or

FYI

If you have a triple-burger-and-fries attack, don't panic. Occasional splurges are OK, just use some damage control. Eat lighter, lower-fat foods at the next meal, and take a good, long walk.

processed foods at your next meal, and by all means, keep your hands off the salt shaker.

	Sodium (mg)
Quarter-pound hamburger with cheese	1,225
French fries	150
Milk shake	230
Fried chicken (2 pieces)	800

On the Side:

- Go easy on the french fries. Even though they may be cooked in cholesterol-free vegetable oil, this doesn't decrease the total fat. It only changes the type of fat. Ask the server to hold the salt; you'll save a couple hundred milligrams of sodium.

- Keep your spuds simple. The potato itself is a dieter's best friend. However, when you stuff it with cheese or smother it with sour cream, the calories and fat top that of a quarter-pound hamburger. Add veggies, salsa, low-fat dressing, cottage cheese, or yogurt from the salad bar.

	Calories	Fat (g)
Quarter-pound hamburger	445	21
Plain potato (10 oz.)	310	0
Bacon & Cheese Potato	530	18
Cheese Baked Potato	560	23

- When in doubt, head for the salad bar. Use the tips in remedy 30 to build a better salad. Just bypass the taco salads, which can carry several hundred calories and a hefty dose of fat. And don't drown your greens in dressing. The standard two-ounce package of dressing can add 200 to 300 calories. Use the "lite" or reduced-calorie dressings or, for a zesty alternative, use three parts lemon or vinegar to one part oil.

- Don't count french fries, potato chips, and onion rings as your vegetables for the day. Eat plenty of fresh vegetables at your next meal to make up for fast food's low fiber count.

Beverages:

- Fortify your meal with nutrient-packed juice or low-fat milk. Or opt for low-calorie unsweetened ice tea, diet soda, or water. You can splurge sometimes and have one of the new low-fat shakes.

- If you buy regular soda, avoid the "tanker" size containers. The large 32 ounce cola has more calories than a regular burger.

Beverages with ice	Calories
Orange drink, 16 oz.	180
Orange drink, 32 oz.	360
Cola, 12 oz.	190
Cola, 32 oz.	380
Diet cola, 32 oz.	3
Other beverages	
1% low-fat milk, 8 oz.	110
orange juice, 6 oz.	80
vanilla low-fat milk shake	290

Desserts:

- Satisfy your sweet tooth with a low-fat frozen yogurt cone rather than the fried pies or sundaes. Better yet, pick up some fresh or sliced fruit at the salad bar.

	Calories	Fat (g)
Vanilla low-fat frozen yogurt cone	105	1
Fried pie	260	15
Hot fudge sundae	240	3
McDonaldland cookies	290	9

28

BE CHOOSEY WITH CHINESE FOOD.

Chinese food has been making news in recent years. If you think it's because Chinese is one of the world's most healthful cuisines, you'd better put down your chopsticks. The fact is, many popular Chinese dishes are loaded with fat and calories. So says a report by the Center for Science in the Public Interest that suggests that many Chinese dishes have higher levels of fat, sodium, and calories than fast foods.

The report found that the average order of Kung pao chicken has almost as much fat as four McDonalds Quarter Pounders. It rated the highest, with an average of 76 grams of fat and 1,620 calories. In fact, half of the meals contained 50 or more grams of fat.

The problem with Chinese food is that it has become Americanized. Many appetizers are fried or coated in heavy peanut or sesame sauces. Often, entrees are first deep fried then stir fried in a wok. To make matters worse, oversized dinner portions yielding five cups of food are typical. And many people polish off the last grain of rice.

But don't despair. The secret to lighter Chinese meals is to eat more like the way they do in China. Here's how:

- Switch proportions. In China, a ratio of four parts rice to one part topping or entree is typical. So, order an extra portion of steamed rice and vegetables, and take half the main entree home in a doggie bag.

- Use chopsticks. These will help you slow down your rate of eating. And it will allow the oily sauces to fall through the cracks and stay on the plate, where they belong.

- Make special requests. Many chinese dishes are cooked to order, so you can control the amount of fat added. Ask to have your meal lightly stir fried in the least amount of oil possible. To reduce sodium, ask them to "hold the MSG or soy sauce." Each tablespoon of soy sauce has 1,000 milligrams of sodium.

- Start off on the right foot. Ask the server to remove those crispy deep-fried noodles that are standard table accessories in most restaurants. Choose a low-fat appetizer such as wonton soup or steamed dumplings instead.

- Know the best and worst bets by following the handy guide below. You'll find a listing by course, as well as a listing of menu terms that signal a wise choice.

Best-Bet Appetizers
- clear, broth-type soups such as wonton, subgum, or watercress
- hot & sour soup
- steamed dumplings
- steamed dim sum
- teriyaki chicken on skewers

Best-Bet Main Dishes
- Moo goo gai pan
- Vegetarian or chicken chop suey dishes
- Chicken chow mein
- Lo mein dishes
- Chicken with vegetables
- Velvet chicken
- Stir-fried dishes (request less oil)
- Steamed or smoked fish dishes
- All bean curd dishes
- Buddha's Delight

Best-Bet Side Dishes & Toppings
- steamed rice
- lo mein noodles
- vegetarian noodles
- steamed vegetables
- duck, plum, or mustard sauce
- fortune cookies (only 19 calories each)

Best-Bet Menu Terms
- Cantonese
- Cooked in wine
- Simmered
- Steamed
- Roasted
- Hot & spicy tomato sauce
- In velvet sauce
- Sliced (not diced) chicken

29

TAKE YOUR TASTE BUDS SOUTH OF THE BORDER.

Nachos, tacos, fajitas, salsa, burritos. Clearly, Mexican foods have crossed the border to become nearly as all-American as apple pie. Luckily for calorie-conscious eaters, Mexican cuisine is economical, exciting, and loaded with nutritious carbohydrate staples such as corn, beans, rice, and various fresh vegetables and fruits.

The key to lite Mexican eating is to keep it simple. The problems start when people order combo platters and pile up on the fatty "extras," such as cheese, sour cream, and guacamole. Yet, many of the dishes are perfect for slimming down. All you have to do is learn a few rules of thumb.

So, if you love Mexican food but hate the calories, give some of these trimming tips a try:

- Skip the complimentary basket of fried corn tortilla chips. Ask for a basket of steamed corn tortillas instead.

- Use the dip-and-stab tactic if you crave fatty toppings such as sour cream or guacamole. Just have your toppings served on the side—not dumped on the entree. Dip your fork into the topping, then spear your fajita or burrito. You'll leave a lot of the fat behind.

- Add pizzazz, not fat, by topping foods with generous portions of salsa. Salsa has only about eight calories per tablespoon, a dieter's delight.

- Order the corn tortillas; they only have a small amount of fat. Flour tortillas are typically made with one to two teaspoons of lard.

- No Mexican meal is considered complete without beans. Choose the boiled beans (frijoles cocidos) over the refried (frijoles refritos.) Refried beans are usually fried in lard and have more fat and cholesterol than the boiled beans.

- Hold off on the flan (milk and egg custard) and sopapillas (fried pastry) for dessert. Enjoy a great cup of Mexican coffee instead.

To discover the lighter side of Mexican foods, use this menu guide to get started:

Best-Bet Appetizers
- Gazpacho (spicy cold tomato soup)
- Black bean soup
- Cantaloupe soup
- Seviche (raw fish marinated in lime juice)
- Steamed corn tortillas with salsa
- Salads (without the fried shells or chips)

Best-Bet Side Dishes and Toppings
- Frijoles cocidos (boiled, not refried, beans)
- Spanish or Mexican rice
- Corn tortillas
- Black beans
- Salsa
- Picante sauce

Best-Bet Main Dishes
- Seafood, chicken, or vegetarian fajitas, enchiladas, tostados, and burritos (request toppings and cheese on the side)
- Arroz con pollo (chicken with rice)
- Chicken or shrimp kebobs
- Grilled fish or chicken entrees
- Chili with beans

30

BUILD A BETTER SALAD.

In search of a "lite" lunch, many dieters bypass the burgers and fries for all-you-can-eat salad bars or chef salads. Unfortunately, their salad-bar choices often look like an edible Leaning Tower of Pisa—fatty meats, cheeses, and coleslaw supported by a wall of potato salad. Even worse, some chef salads can weigh in at about 1,200 calories and 60 percent fat. What's a salad lover to do? Keep salads healthy and low fat. Fortunately, there are many great options. You just have to know what to look for.

Undressing Your Salad for Success

Drowning your salad greens in a sea of dressing defeats the purpose of a low-fat salad. Each tablespoon of regular salad dressing typically has about 75 calories, approximately 90 percent of them from fat. And one small restaurant ladle holds about two tablespoons, or about 150 calories worth, of dressing. To put this in perspective, two tablespoons of dressing have as many calories as one slice of cheese pizza. And some people pour about ¼ cup (300 calories) to ½ cup (600 calories) of dressing onto their eight-calorie cup of iceberg lettuce. As you can see, dressing your salad for success can make a big fat difference. Here are some simple salad tips:

- Pour on the flavor, not the fat, by using lemon juice, flavored vinegars, and herbs.

- Trade in the ladle for a tablespoon measure. Dress your salad with not more than two level, not heaping, tablespoons of reduced-calorie dressing. Switching to a reduced-calorie dressing will save about seven grams of fat per tablespoon. Better yet, try some of the new no-oil dressings.

- Stretch the fat in your favorite dressings. Mix creamy dressings with buttermilk or low-fat yogurt. Thin others with lemon juice, vinegar, or water. You'll keep the taste but cut the calories and fat by about 50 percent.

- Ask for your dressing on the side so you can use the dip-and-stab technique. Dip your fork into the dressing, then stab some lettuce. You'll get all the flavor but leave lots of fat behind.

- Beware the packets of dressing at fast-food spots. One packet typically holds four tablespoons of dressing. That's 300 to 400 calories just in the dressing—about 90 percent of them from fat.

- At home, put your thinner dressings in a spray bottle. Spray, rather than pour, dressings. You'll not only get better salad coverage, but you'll cut the fat by 50 percent or more.

- Know how your favorite dressings stack up:

	Dressings (2 tbsp.)	Fat (g)	Calories
Fill up on...	Vinegar (any type)	0	2
	Lemon or lime juice	0	6
	No-oil dressings	4	0
	Low-calorie dressings		
	Blue cheese	4	54
	French	2	44
	Italian	3	32
	Russian	1	46
	Thousand Island	3	48
	Yogurt, nonfat plain	<1	13
	Yogurt, low-fat plain	<1	15
Go easy on...	Blue cheese	16	154
	French	13	134
	Italian	14	137
	Ranch	16	156
	Russian	16	152
	Thousand Island	11	118
	Vinegar and oil	16	144

FYI

A small restaurant ladle of salad dressing holds about two tablespoons. A regular ladle holds about four tablespoons, or 300 calories worth, of dressing.

Choose Healthier Salad Ingredients

Once you have your dressings under control, it's time to build a better salad. Remember, salads are an easy way to have one or more of the recommended five servings of fruits and vegetables a day. Here are some trimming tips:

- At the salad bar, use a smaller plate so that the amount of food you take will look like more. Usually, there are dinner and dessert plates available. Remember, many times we fill our plates out of habit not hunger.

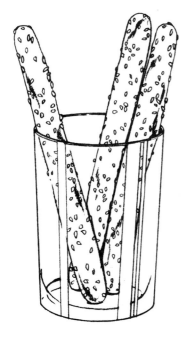

- Defat your salad by going easy on the creamy and oily premixed salads. The potato salad, coleslaw, macaroni salad, and tuna, chicken, or seafood salads can make fat skyrocket. So if you love these mixtures, be sure to practice some portion control.

- Go for color. In general, the darker the vegetable, the higher the nutrient content. Romaine lettuce, for example, has six times as much vitamin C and eight times as much vitamin A by weight as pale iceberg lettuce.

- Keep it simple. Grab a few bread sticks, melba toast, or regular bread (without butter). Pass up the garlic bread dripping in oil and the corn bread as well as other fancy breads and muffins.

- Limit yourself to just one salad-bar trip. If your stomach cries for more, wait five minutes. You may discover that you're fuller than you think.

- At home, dry lettuce thoroughly by spinning in a salad spinner or patting with paper towels. Wet lettuce will not hold dressing, and you'll wind up using twice as much.

- Fill up on healthy salad-bar ingredients. To find your best bets, use the accompanying chart of salad ingredients.

	Salad ingredients	Average grams of fat	Average calories
Fill up on...	Alfalfa sprouts, 2 tbsp.	0	2
	Broccoli, ⅓ cup	<1	6
	Cucumber, 6 slices	<1	2
	Cauliflower, ⅓ cup	<1	8
	Carrots, grated, 2 tbsp.	<1	6
	Fresh fruit salad, ½ cup	<1	50
	Garbanzo beans, 2 tbsp.	<1	34
	Green peppers, 2 tbsp.	<1	3
	Kidney beans, 2 tbsp.	<1	28
	Lettuce, 1 cup	<1	8
	Mushrooms, 2 tbsp.	<1	2
	Spinach, raw, 1 cup	<1	12
	Tomato, ½ whole	<1	12
	Turkey, ⅓ cup	<1	73

Go easy on...

Bacon bits, 2 tbsp.	3	61
Canned fruit, ½ cup	0	100
Coleslaw, mayonnaise type, ⅓ cup	6	67
Cheddar cheese, shredded, 2 tbsp.	5	57
Croutons, 2 tbsp.	1	22
Macaroni salad, mayonnaise type, ⅓ cup	6	120
Potato salad, mayonnaise type, ⅓ cup	6	113
Olives, black, chopped, 2 tbsp.	2	19
Parmesan cheese, 2 tbsp.	3	46
Sunflower seeds, 2 tbsp.	8	93
Avocado, ¼ cup	9	90

31

HAVE A HEALTHY HAPPY HOUR.

Alcohol works against weight loss and can set you up to fail. There are four big reasons why you should limit alcohol consumption as much as possible while you're trying to lose weight:

1. Alcohol adds calories fast, and they're empty calories. For example, if you drink one can of beer a day in excess of your normal caloric needs, you could gain 15 pounds in one year. A glass of wine every day could add ten pounds.

2. Recent studies show that alcohol causes your body to burn less fat—so fat-burning and weight loss slow down.

3. Alcohol lowers your blood-sugar level, which can make you feel hungry and prompt you to eat more. To put it simply, alcohol stimulates your appetite.

4. Alcohol distorts your judgment and dissolves your restraint about overeating.

That's not to say a toast or two once in a while will ruin your diet. The more you know about what you choose to drink, the easier it is for you to exercise your options. Here are some tips for how you can drink and be merry without blowing your diet:

- Try a "mocktail" (a drink without alcohol). Ask for fruit juice mixed with seltzer or mineral water, a margarita minus the booze, or tomato juice with a twist of lime or lemon. Or have the ideal thirst quencher—water! Give your mocktails a festive flair by using garnishes and stirrers. At least you'll have a glass in your hand to ward off anyone who might encourage you to have an alcoholic drink.

- Alternate drinks. This simply means never having two drinks containing alcohol in a row. For example, you can trade off one mixed drink, one club soda, one mixed drink, one club soda. This slows down even the heartiest drinker.

- Stretch the calories in wine by having a wine spritzer (wine and seltzer water). Twelve ounces has only about 125 calories, while the same amount of wine alone will cost you 240 calories. Don't be fooled by wine coolers, which are made with regular soda and run about 215 calories. If you order wine, stick with a glass rather than a carafe.

- Order a mixed drink made with half the usual amount of alcohol and plenty of ice. To control calories and sugar, request liquor mixed with water or seltzer rather than sweetened mixers.

- The higher the proof of alcohol, the higher the calories. For a refreshing change, why not try some of the popular alcohol-free or light wines and beers?

- The number of calories in two drinks can equal the number of calories in a rich dessert. So, trade off alcohol calories for other extras. For example, if you have an alcoholic beverage, pass on the dessert, the appetizer, or the butter added to your bread. You just can't have it all.

- Volunteer to be the designated driver. You'll not only save calories, you may also save someone's life.

- Know the number of calories you'll be drinking in by using the chart below.

THE PRICE YOU PAY FOR ALCOHOL

Drinks	Approximate Calories	Drinks	Approximate Calories
Beer		*Wine*	
Regular beer, 12 fl. oz.	150	Champagne, dry, 5 fl. oz.	133
Light beer, 12 fl. oz.	100	Sweet, 5 fl. oz.	225
Alcohol-free beer, 12 fl. oz.	60	Dry table, red, 5 fl. oz.	105
		Dry table, white, 5 fl. oz.	100
Liquor			
Cordials, liqueurs, 1 oz.	80-120	*Mixed Drinks*	
Gin, rum, vodka, or whiskey,		Bloody Mary, 5 fl. oz.	116
86 proof, 1 jigger	105	Gin and tonic, 8 fl. oz.	182
Vermouth, sweet, 1 jigger	70	Manhattan, 4 fl. oz.	255
Vermouth, dry, 1 jigger	55	Martini, 4 fl. oz.	249
		Scotch and soda, 4 fl. oz.	97
		Whiskey sour, 4 fl. oz.	180

32

"JUST SAY NO" TO GET WHAT YOU WANT.

One of the most important social skills you need while losing weight is the ability to say no to food—and to make it stick.

Many people are afraid to say no. They don't want to refuse someone's offer of food because they're afraid of hurting the other person's feelings. Wanting to be polite, wanting the other person's approval, or feeling sorry for the other person may pressure them into accepting an offer of food even if they don't want it.

Your best approach? To communicate clearly, objectively, and politely with the person who is offering the food. Have and rehearse a ready response for when someone offers food. Stand in front of the mirror and act out the script with the ending you choose. Remember, you only have to say "No, thanks" one more time than they say "Here, have some." Here are a few lines you can use:

• "No thanks. I've had enough, but I'd really appreciate it if you could give me the recipe."

• "Oh, I absolutely love your cakes, but I have to take a rain check this time."

• "They're my all-time favorites. The fact is I'm trying to lose weight, and I'd love your support. Please help by not offering food."

• "That's so thoughtful of you. Sorry, I'll have to pass, because I just had lunch."

• "It looks so wonderful, but I'm too full to eat another bite. Can I save one for later?"

These are just a few suggestions. Why not try to develop some of your own? Remember, you're doing something good for yourself when you decide to control your weight, so make it as easy on yourself as possible. When saying no, keep the following points in mind:

- You have the right to say no.

- Saying no to offers of food doesn't mean that you're rejecting the person who is making the offer. You're simply rejecting a request or behavior.

- Saying no doesn't mean you're rude, impolite, or selfish.

- When saying no, be concise and to the point.

- By all means, offer reasons for refusing the offer, but don't get carried away with numerous "excuses."

- Saying no without guilt can become a habit...one that can be growth-enhancing, weight-reducing, and healthy. Practice it so that you become a pro. And remember that you are in the process of doing something that is beneficial to you.

33

PUMP UP YOUR EFFORTS WITH POSITIVE SELF-TALK.

What do your thoughts have to do with weight loss? Plenty. We talk to ourselves all the time. We call this silent conversation that we have with ourselves "self-talk." And what we say influences what we do...including whether or not we lose weight.

Self-talk is very powerful. By repeating the same thoughts over and over, the mind actually comes to believe they're true. We tend to act in ways consistent with our deepest internal beliefs. So, frequently, the statements become self-fulfilling. For example, if you tell yourself every day that losing weight is hopeless, eventually you will feel powerless to make changes. Simply put, you can talk yourself into doing something—such as losing weight—or talk yourself out of it.

How's your self-talk? Listen to that voice in the back of your head. Is it positive and moving you toward your goals? Or is it destructive and undermining your weight-control efforts? Remember, even negative self-talk can be changed by positive thinking.

Here are a few examples of how you can change your self-talk so that it works for, not against, your weight-control efforts.

WHAT DO YOU SAY ABOUT YOUR WEIGHT-CONTROL EFFORTS?

Negative Self-Talk	Positive Self-Talk
I'm a hopeless failure. It's been over a week, and I haven't lost a pound.	I may not have lost weight, but I did exercise and plan my meals. If I keep making these small changes, I'll reach my goals.
My mother and father are both overweight. I guess I'll always be fat because it's in my genes.	My genes aren't my destiny. I know I can lose weight with healtier habits.
It's not fair that I have to eat diet food when everyone else can eat what they want.	Lots of people are watching what they eat. I'm not alone in choosing healthful, nutritious foods that my body deserves.

It's time for my daily punishment for being fat. I have to go to the gym.

Once I finish exercising, I always feel re-energized and in control.

I have no willpower.

Weight loss takes skillpower, not willpower. By identifying my habits, planning ahead, and thinking positively, I can tackle my weight problem.

Life is no fun when I'm on a diet.

I make my own fun through friends and activities. Food is only fuel for my body.

As you can see, positive self-talk is a valuable skill that will enhance your self-image and lower the barriers between you and your goals. While you're learning this skill, write down your self-talk. You can use a diary similar to the one in remedy 36. It will help you to think more objectively about yourself and your weight-loss efforts.

You can also use your diary to record a mental inventory of your successes at the end of each day. What did you do well? Focus on the positive ("I went for a walk three times this week and felt great!"), not on the negative ("I missed walking one day.") And think about how you can make tomorrow better. Be sure to praise yourself for every one of your successes, even if they seem small.

Remember, weight control is much easier if you believe you can do it. Many of us have some doubts about reaching our goals, and this is natural. But by replacing our doubts with positive thoughts, we build belief in ourselves. And that belief can help us achieve our goals.

34

CONQUER URGES WITH CALORIE-FREE BREAKS.

A mouthful of chocolate candy, a sliver of cake, a chunk of cheese... give into those insistent urges, and before you know it, you've eaten everything but the kitchen sink. Even worse, those little urges can

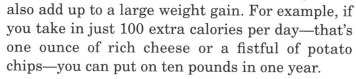

also add up to a large weight gain. For example, if you take in just 100 extra calories per day—that's one ounce of rich cheese or a fistful of potato chips—you can put on ten pounds in one year.

So, when the urge to eat strikes, stop and ask yourself if you're really hungry. If not, then you're merely eating out of habit, and the urge will usually pass if you can wait it out.

Overcoming the eating urge can be compared to riding a bucking bronco. You can fight the horse and be thrown or maintain your balance and "ride" the horse until it settles down. Being a good "urge rider" involves identifying your urges early and using skills to ride them through. One skill to "ride out" your urges is to distract yourself for at least ten minutes with activities that are incompatible with eating. The goal is to "buy time" and choose activities that meet several criteria: They must involve you, be readily available, and give you pleasure or fill you with a sense of accomplishment. Here are some activity suggestions to get you started, but it's important to create your own list:

- Call a friend (don't use the phone in the kitchen)
- Chew a wad of sugarless gum
- Brush your teeth
- Take a shower
- Paint your nails
- Water your plants
- Ride your exercise bike
- Organize your closet
- Read this book

- Complete your food diary
- Meditate, pray, or think pleasant thoughts (but not about food)
- File papers or balance your checkbook
- Grab your mate, not your plate
- Work on a crossword puzzle or a jigsaw puzzle

Do not use television as your alternate activity. Studies show that obesity is almost twice as common in people who watch three to four hours of television daily as in those who watch less than one hour. This fatty connection may be due to the decrease in activity and the mindless snacking that tends to go hand in hand with watching television. If you watch four hours of television every day, that adds up to 1,460 hours each year. Just think of all the useful or enjoyable things you could do with those hours instead.

Another way to ride out your urges is to change your environment. If you're alone, visit a friend (who won't offer you food.) If you're working overtime, take "seventh-inning stretches" in hallways. If you're in the kitchen, go to the bedroom or living room with a good book. Once you leave the environment, especially if it contained food, your desire to eat will eventually weaken.

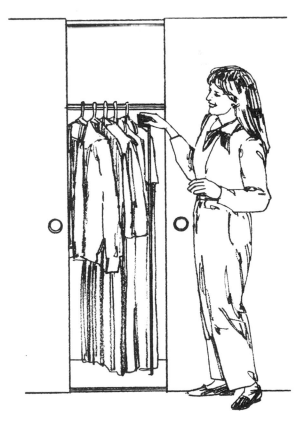

When you just can't resist an urge to eat, simply satisfy it with low-calorie foods and beverages. This is easy to do if you have an emergency stash of low-calorie items on hand, such as fresh vegetables, fruit, diet soda, and air-popped popcorn.

Finally, ask yourself if your urges are simply a sign of fatigue. Many people feel like eating when they are tired, run-down, or sick. Once you recognize when you're tired, you can step off the treadmill and give your body what it really wants—a little break. And don't feel guilty taking the extra time. If you ride out urges productively, you'll be surprised at the free time you have that once was filled with mindless eating.

35

SET REALISTIC GOALS THAT DON'T RIVAL MOUNT EVEREST.

How many times have you started a new year or a Monday morning with resolutions like this:

"I'm going to exercise every day."
"I will never eat chocolate or desserts again!"
"I have to lose ten pounds in two weeks."

Often, dieters set up "no-win" situations for themselves by having unrealistic expectations about how "perfect" they can be and how much weight they can lose. These statements may seem innocent, but if they form the foundation of the way you approach goals, you are in store for serious disappointment.

The best way to avoid disappointment is to learn how to set goals you can attain. When learning this skill, there are two common pitfalls most dieters encounter: The Insistent Imperatives and The Mount Everest Syndrome. By knowing these pitfalls, you can be prepared to sidestep them.

The Insistent Imperatives

Many dieters have goals filled with imperative words that leave no room for error and imply demand, such as "always," "never," "every," and "must." Despite what many of us like to think, nobody's perfect. So every time you vow never to touch a doughnut again or swear that you'll lose weight every week or promise that you'll always control your eating—you're setting yourself up to fail by insisting on perfection. To make matters worse, if you violate your own rigid standards, you will be disappointed in yourself and may eat even more because you feel so frustrated.

Remember that to err is human—everyone has setbacks. So, strike imperatives from your vocabulary. If you bring your standards in line with reality, you'll be regularly rewarded instead of frustrated.

The Mount Everest Syndrome

The second trap dieters fall into is creating goals the size of Mount Everest—"I need to lose 50 pounds" or "I'm going to walk ten miles." Giant goals like these are overwhelming because of the size of the job and the time it will take to do it. Even worse, this type of thinking can lead to despair because it sets up success as an endpoint that happens only when the goal is achieved rather than as a continuing process.

Granted, your goals should be challenging, but giant goals are an invitation to failure. That's why it's so important to break goals down into smaller tasks that you can accomplish one day or one week at a time so you won't feel defeated before you start.

Steps for Setting Goals

Goals are important because they help you focus your time and energy on the areas that count. To set yourself up to succeed, your goals should be:

Short term and specific. Specify exactly what you plan to do by tomorrow or next week. Say "I'm going to walk 25 minutes after dinner every evening this week," rather than "I'm going to exercise."

Trackable. Use a diary to track your progress in a visible way. See remedy 36 for more on using a diary to monitor your progress toward reaching your goals.

Positive. Say "I will" rather than "I won't." Negative goals make you feel deprived instead of making you feel good about your successes.

Personal. Don't try to lose weight to please or impress others. Learn to be the center of your own life.

Rewarding. Recognize each small victory. They are your building blocks for long-term success.

Realistic. In order to achieve long-term success, you have to find goals you can live with and incorporate into your daily schedule. On the following page, you'll find examples of unrealistic goals that can sabotage your weight-loss efforts, as well as sample realistic goals that can fuel your weight-loss efforts.

Unrealistic goals	Realistic goals
I'll never eat more than 1,000 calories every day.	My average daily intake will be 1,500 calories this week.
Starting tomorrow, I'm going to begin walking two hours every day.	I'll walk for 20 minutes four times this week.
I'm going to bake cookies for the bake sale, and I won't eat or taste any.	I'll buy cookies for the bake sale and drop them off at the school on my way home from the grocery store.
I'm going to lose ten pounds before my class reunion next month.	I'm going to eat small portions and take a 15-minute walk four times a week so that I'll feel healthier, more fit, and confident at the class reunion.

Be sure to write your goals down. Then read them over to be sure they fit the description of realistic goals. If you catch yourself using imperatives or asking yourself to be perfect, revise your thinking and your goals.

36

USE A DIARY TO END DIETER'S AMNESIA.

Losing weight is the easy part when we consider lifestyle change. Keeping lost weight from finding you again is the single biggest challenge facing today's dieter. Does anything help? The answer from researchers at the Duke University Diet & Fitness Center is a resounding yes. Studies of successful "losers" show that they developed a habit of keeping a daily diary.

Diary keeping seems to aid weight control in three ways.

1. **Focus:** Daily diary keeping helps individuals remind themselves of, and focus on, the importance of their personal health goals.

2. **Plan:** Failure to plan regular meals and daily physical activity is the single biggest pitfall dieters face when attempting to make lifestyle changes. A goal without a plan is just a wish...and we all know that wishing doesn't make it so. Plan meals and fitness activity at least a day, preferably a week, ahead of time. Make your plan a realistic one that considers your other activities and responsibilities. Once you have a plan, stick to it. If you do deviate from your plan, write it down. Include things like when and where it happened and who you were with. Later, you can use such information to help you identify, and prepare for, high-risk situations.

3. **Reflection:** Keeping a daily diary is an extremely important tool for self-monitoring. Your diary will help you see patterns in your behavior that are moving you toward, or away from, your goals. Remember, it's important to monitor and praise yourself for progress in areas other than just weight.

Use the following sample diary pages to track some of the same areas Duke University Diet & Fitness Center All-Stars track. You'll find extra diary pages in the appendix, as well.

Date_____ Daily Record

MEAL PLAN

FOOD	PORTION	CALORIES	FAT (G)
BREAKFAST			
		Total Calories_____	
LUNCH			
		Total Calories_____	
DINNER			
		Total Calories_____	

PLANNED EATING   Total Calories_____

UNPLANNED EATING

TIME	FOOD	CALORIES	SITUATION/FEELINGS

Total Daily Calories_____
(Include any calories from unplanned eating)

EXERCISE PLAN

ACTIVITY	DURATION	COMMENTS

Aerobic:

Strength:

Stretching:

THINKING ABOUT TODAY

How I felt about myself today:

What I did well today:

How I can make tomorrow better:

"A goal without a plan is just a wish"

37

EAT SLOWLY TO FEEL FULLER.

Both laboratory and clinical studies confirm that eating slowly leads to greater satisfaction from less food. It takes about 20 minutes for your brain to tell your stomach you have had enough to eat. If you slow down, signals of fullness will kick in and curb your desire for second helpings. So give your brain and stomach time to get in "sync." You'll taste your food more, enjoy it more, and finish when everyone else does.

If you're breaking speed records at meals, consider these techniques to slow down:

- Put your fork or spoon down after every bite. For many people, eating is a nonstop motion: The fork or spoon is racing from plate to mouth. The trick is to take a spoonful of food, put the spoon down beside your plate, chew, swallow, then pick up the spoon again. At first, this will feel awkward and tedious. But you'll be surprised how much sooner you'll feel full.

- Swallow what is in your mouth before preparing the next bite. Many people are busy loading up their utensils while their mouth is still filled.

- If you're eating hand-held food—such as pizza, sandwiches, bagels, or cookies—take one bite, then put the rest of your food down while you chew.

- Relax before you start eating. If you're upset over a problem at work or if the kids are fighting, do some deep breathing or read the paper to settle down. The key is to calm down first and then start eating at a leisurely pace.

- Eat your meal in courses, rather than family style where all the foods are on the table at the same time.

- Time your meals with a watch or kitchen timer until you get used to the slower pace.

- Take a brief break for a minute once or twice during the meal. Talk, sip a beverage, or fold your hands in your lap.

- Play slow background music. Studies have shown that people eat more slowly when they listen to slow, soft music.

- When it's time to eat, do nothing but eat. Devote your full attention to the meal. Make it a habit to turn off the television and take the phone off the hook. If you're distracted by other activities, you may not notice how fast you are eating.

- Use chopsticks for all cuisines. They automatically slow down your rate of eating and the amount of food you're going to eat. If you're a pro with chopsticks, however, use them in the opposite hand! As an added bonus, chopsticks allow the fatty sauces to fall through the cracks and stay on the plate where they belong.

- Sit down when you eat. This helps you relax and focus on eating. A lot of people simply don't count what they eat when they are standing up.

- Dine— don't just "inhale" your food. For example, you can savor each delicious bite of tuna salad on a fresh bed of leafy greens, or you can "wolf" your tuna fish right out of the can. Why not make mealtime a pleasurable event?

- Finally, be creative, and develop your own tricks for slowing down your eating.

38

GET A LITTLE HELP FROM YOUR FRIENDS.

Losing weight is much easier if you build a team of people you can turn to for support, comfort, understanding, or helpful ideas. Here are some effective strategies for evaluating and building the social support in your life:

Step 1: Evaluate your social network.

Identify your allies—people who'll support your weight-loss efforts—and your saboteurs—those who might undermine your efforts. The most obvious place to start looking for your allies is in your family, but friends and coworkers can also be allies.

Spend time with those who'll help, not hinder, your efforts. For example, if you're trying to cut back on calories, don't meet Jane the food-pusher or your drinking buddies after work. Meet with people who'll exercise with you and reinforce your efforts.

Step 2: Tell allies how to help.

Other people can't read your mind. The only way to get what you want is to ask for it. So be clear about how you want others to support you. Requests such as "Help me out more" or "You're making it impossible for me to lose weight" are too vague.

Here are a few examples of specific things that you might ask your allies to do:

To provide daily encouragement and support:

- Ask them to praise behavior changes not weight loss. Positive feedback shouldn't depend on weight loss, because it may be slow at times. Positive behavior changes, such as eating slowly or revising recipes, can occur at any time and deserve support.

- Ask them to avoid criticizing your efforts even if you fall off your plan.

- Ask them to call or talk to you and explore solutions with you when you're having trouble with your plan.

- Ask them to walk or exercise with you. Sharing an activity can replace the usual eating ritual of most social get-togethers.

To reduce your exposure to food:

- Ask them to avoid offering you food or giving you food as a gift. Assure them you'll ask for what you want to eat.

- Ask them to avoid eating "problem" foods in your presence.

- Ask them to clear the table and put food away as soon as the meal is over.

- Ask them to store food out of sight in the kitchen.

To reduce the importance of food:

- Ask them to minimize "food talk" with you.

- Ask them to demonstrate affection with hugs, kisses, or words—not food.

- Ask them to invite you to activities that don't revolve around eating—such as movies, plays, or sporting events.

- Ask them to entertain with reduced-fat foods.

With such clear-cut suggestions, people close to you will be able to support you. In the past, they may have felt left out or didn't think you wanted their help, because you never told them exactly what you needed.

When people help you, don't just thank them. Acknowledge the specific behavior you would like repeated, as well. For example, you might say something like "Thanks for not buying ice cream. It really helps when it's not in the house." Don't be too general and say, "Thanks for being so helpful." And be sure to ask what you can do for them in return—helping is a two-way street.

39

KEEP THE MUSCLE, LOSE THE FAT.

Despite what you thought when you bought this book, you aren't reading this book just to lose weight. You're reading this book to lose excess body fat. Our goal is to ensure that the weight that you lose will be high quality—primarily fat, and not muscle. You're ensured of losing mostly fat in two ways:

1. **Gradual weight loss.** Weight loss can be dangerous if too much muscle is sacrificed. When you lose weight too rapidly, you lose muscle tissue. And muscle tissue can be lost from almost every part of your body—potentially even your heart. Gradual weight loss generally means losing no more than one to two pounds per week.

2. **Regular exercise.** The golden rule with muscle is "use it or lose it." Exercise preserves precious muscle tissue.

Exercise is the single most important factor in long-term weight management. Here's why:

Exercise maintains or increases muscle mass. Muscle is very active tissue; that means it burns fuel even when you're sitting or sleeping. Think of your lean muscle tissue as your body's engine. The larger the engine, the more gas it burns. The larger your muscle mass, the more calories you burn. If you lose muscle tissue, your "engine" becomes smaller and you need less "gas," or fewer calories, to keep it running. Such a loss of muscle reduces your daily calorie needs.

Exercise keeps your daily energy needs elevated. Because exercise can preserve, or even increase, active muscle tissue, it has a direct, positive impact on your daily energy needs. In this way, it increases your energy demands both at work and at rest.

Exercise helps you lose weight without feeling deprived. Many people mistakenly fear that exercise will make them hungry, so they'll eat more and gain weight. Numerous studies show that a program of moderate exercise barely increases food intake. The result? Weight loss without feelings of deprivation.

Exercise helps to regulate your appetite. A growing body of research has shown that people who exercise regularly seem to automatically select foods that are higher in complex carbohydrate over foods that are high in fat.

Exercise helps you feel better. Keeping active and shaping up can make you feel like a new person. You'll feel less tense and better able to cope with daily stress. You'll improve the quality of your sleep at night and your energy level during the day. And you'll improve your self-image.

40

STRIVE FOR CONSISTENCY, NOT INTENSITY.

People who believe in "no pain, no gain" have it all wrong. Medical studies show that when it comes to health, consistency of exercise is much more important than intensity.

In fact, in 1993, the American College of Sports Medicine issued new exercise guidelines that are within reach for just about everyone. They state: "Adult Americans should accumulate 30 minutes or more of moderate intensity physical activity during the course of most days." What's new about these guidelines is that the 30 minutes of activity doesn't have to happen at the same time. And it need not be strenuous. So, a ten-minute walk in the morning, five minutes of raking leaves in the afternoon, and a 15-minute ride on a stationary bike in the evening would meet the recommendations.

What does this mean for you? You don't have to be a runner or even an athlete to gain the benefits of exercise. All activity counts. By adding just a little more activity to your daily life, you can greatly improve your health and weight in the long run. Whether you're taking a walk around the shopping mall or pushing the lawn mower around, there are a number of simple ways that you can activate your day (see remedy 45). Remember, the best exercise isn't necessarily the most strenuous—it's the one you enjoy the most, because that's the kind of exercise you'll be more likely to stick with.

41

TAKE A WALK FOR ALL GAIN, NO PAIN.

It isn't necessary to suffer through shinsplints, tennis elbow, marathon mania, or aerobic-dance fever to lose weight. All you need to do is start walking. And you won't be alone. Some 67 million Americans walk regularly. In fact, walking has earned a special reputation with weight watchers for these reasons:

It shapes you up. Walking strengthens and tones your abdomen, hips, buttocks, arms, shoulders, calves, thighs, ankles—even your feet. It burns calories. Since moderately brisk walking burns about 100 calories per mile, if you walked an extra mile each day, over the course of a year you'd burn off about 36,500 calories—or the equivalent of about ten pounds.

It's virtually injury free. Unlike jogging or aerobics, which can produce an impact roughly three to four times your body weight when each foot hits the ground, walking reduces the impact to about 1 to 1½ times your body weight.

It can help relieve stress and takes you away from eating. Walking can help prevent stress-induced overeating. The longer you walk, the longer you'll be away from food.

It burns fat. Walking uses lots of oxygen and it works the large muscle groups, thereby turning on your body's fat-burning power. If you pump your arms as you stride along, you'll burn even more calories.

It's healthy, convenient, fun, economical, and probably the world's most underrated sport. Walking also leads to cardiovascular fitness and lower blood pressure.

To lose weight, it's more important to walk longer than harder. For instance, you are better off walking a longer distance for 25 minutes at a slower pace than trying to jog, getting tired, and quitting after only ten minutes. In fact, you burn almost the same number of calories whether you walk or run a mile—it just takes longer to walk the mile than run it.

In order to get the most from your walking workout, here are a few pointers:

- Be sure to warm up and cool down. Walk slowly for five minutes (to warm up); walk briskly for 20 minutes (aerobic exercise); and walk slowly for five minutes (to cool down).

- Stand tall. Hold your head high, and walk with your rib cage up and shoulders back.

- Bend your elbows at a 90-degree angle (so that each arm forms an "L"), and make a slight pumping action with your arms as you walk. Not only will you end up walking faster, you'll burn five to ten percent more calories.

- Stride smoothly. Plant your heel so that your foot is at a 90-degree angle to your leg. The back of the heel should strike first, and your weight should roll forward so that you end each step by pushing off with your toes.

- Wear a comfortable walking shoe that provides adequate support and cushioning. And never wear ankle weights, which can alter your gait.

42

LIVE THE F.I.T. LIFE.

Imagine yourself waking up each morning eager to go out for your daily exercise. Sound like a dream? Consider this: Just as it's possible to develop bad habits, it's possible to develop good habits, habits that move you toward your weight-loss goals. In fact, numerous studies show that exercise is one of the best predictors of weight-loss maintenance.

One of the most important types of exercise for weight control is aerobic exercise, such as walking, jogging, biking, and cross-country skiing. Many people find this type of exercise especially habit forming because of the great feeling they experience afterward. Not only can it help you feel better, aerobic exercise plays a key role in strengthening your heart and lungs. However, the most important role of aerobic exercise in controlling weight is its potential for burning stored body fat.

The word aerobic means "with oxygen." This type of exercise brings oxygen to your muscles to burn stored fuel for energy. Just as oxygen feeds a campfire's flames, the oxygen you breathe keeps your body's furnace going. Instead of wood logs, your body burns "fat logs," which provide the energy necessary to sustain physical activity over long periods of time.

Aerobic exercise is important when you are trying to lose weight because it targets your fat stores, providing fuel for active muscles. That's why, as you become increasingly fit, you become a better fat burner.

Let the acronym **F.I.T.** help you remember how to improve your aerobic fitness.

F = Frequency: Exercise three to five times per week. Start out gradually, and increase the number of days per week that you exercise as you become more fit.

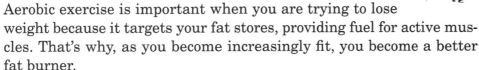

I = Intensity: Exercise at a comfortable level within your heart-rate target zone. Use your heart rate or the "talk/sing" test to determine if you are exercising in your target zone. See remedy 43 for more information on checking your heart rate and taking the "talk/sing" test.

T = Time: Exercise for 20 to 30 minutes to improve your weight-control efforts. Your sessions may be continuous (20 minutes of nonstop activity) or intermittent (two 10-minute sessions). Both approaches yield health benefits.

For any activity to be considered aerobic, it must meet the F.I.T. principles, and it should involve the largest muscle groups in your body—the ones below your waist.

One final note: Don't let these rules intimidate you. Activity doesn't have to be hard or intense to be beneficial. The consistency of the activity is most important. Remember, your body reaps rewards whenever you get up and get moving!

43

MAKE YOUR MOVES TO A BETTER BEAT.

How hard should you exercise? Believe it or not, your voice and your fingertips are wonderful devices for finding the answer to this fitness question. Simply take the talk/sing test and check your heart rate, or pulse, as you exercise.

During exercise, you should be able to breathe comfortably and talk. Talking shows that you are able to effectively deliver oxygen to all the muscles you are working. If you are gasping for air, you are working too hard. Slow down. On the other hand, if you can sing "The Star-Spangled Banner," then you're going too slow. You should increase the intensity at which you are exercising.

You can also determine how hard you should be working during exercise by keeping track of your heart rate. Your maximum heart rate is the fastest your heart can beat. The preferred activity level is 60 percent to 75 percent of this maximum rate. This range is called your heart-rate target zone.

When you begin an exercise program, aim for the lower part of your target zone (60 percent) during the first few months. As you get in better shape, gradually build up to the higher part of your target zone (75 percent).

Find your target zone in the table on the next page by looking for the age closest to your own and reading across the line. For example, if you are 43 years of age, the closest age is 45; your heart-rate target zone during exercise is 105 to 131 beats per minute.

When working out, give yourself time to raise your heart rate. Then check your pulse during the routine to see if it's in your target zone. To check your pulse, place the index and middle finger of one hand on the underside of the wrist of the other hand. You should be able to feel your pulse just below the heel of the hand. (If you don't feel your pulse right away, adjust the position of your fingers until you can feel the beats.) Count the beats for 15 seconds. Multiply the number of beats by four. If your pulse falls below your target zone, exercise a little harder. If your pulse is above your target zone, ease up.

It is important to note that if you are taking heart or blood-pressure medication, your heart rate may be lowered, and you should talk to your doctor before beginning an exercise program. Likewise, you should check with your doctor before beginning an exercise program if you smoke, are over 45 years of age and have never exercised regularly, or have a chronic medical condition such as diabetes, heart disease, high blood pressure, or kidney disease.

HEART-RATE TARGET ZONES

Age (years)	Target Zone (beats per minute)
20	120–150
25	117–146
30	114–142
35	111–138
40	108–135
45	105–131
50	102–127
55	99–120
60	93–116
70	90–113

44

WEATHERIZE YOUR EXERCISE.

Keeping fit is a year-round pursuit. Yet, when the mercury soars to 90 degrees Fahrenheit or dives down into single digits, even the most die-hard fitness fans can shy away from exercising. Here's some good news. Neither rain, nor sleet, nor snow will stop you from staying active—if you exercise your options.

When the heat is on...

- Exercise in the early morning or evening hours; the temperature is likely to be cooler. And try to cut your level of exercise back for a week to acclimate your body to the change in temperature.

- Wear loose-fitting, lightweight, light-colored clothing. Avoid plastic suits or other clothes designed to make you sweat and lose weight "faster." These devices can be dangerous because they cause over-heating. Just remember, any weight loss from sweating is only a water loss, not a loss of fat. The water lost will be regained as soon as you have anything to drink or eat.

- Drink lots of fluids before, during, and after exercise to prevent de-hydration. Here are a few tips for maximizing your liquid assets:

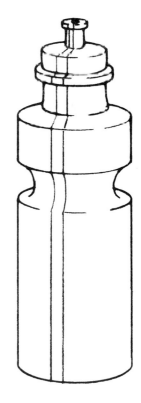

  Drink before you feel thirsty. Remember, thirst can be a poor indicator of your fluid needs.

  Drink two glasses of water approximately one hour before working out. Drink one glass of water every 15 to 30 minutes while working out. Replenish fluids again—with as much water as you can drink—right after you're finished exercising.

  Don't choose cola, ice tea, iced coffee, or other caffeine- or alcohol-containing beverages to replenish fluids; these beverages can have a dehydrating effect.

  If you exercise vigorously for less than one hour or moderately for less than two hours, opt for water over costly sports drinks. However, if your exercise exceeds these limits, you can benefit from a sports drink during exercise. Keep in mind, sports drinks do rack up a fair amount of calories, mostly in the form of sugar.

Drink cool beverages, because they are absorbed faster than luke-warm fluids.

Carry a water bottle so you can replenish fluids regularly. Remember, water is worth its weight; dehydration is dangerous and exhausting, especially in the heat.

Weigh yourself before and after vigorous activity. For every pound lost through sweat, drink two cups (16 ounces) of water. You don't, however, need extra salt, because your diet probably provides more than enough.

- Watch out for signs of heatstroke—feeling dizzy, weak, light-headed, and/or excessively tired. As heatstroke progresses, sweating stops and body temperature rises excessively high. If you experience any of these symptoms, stop exercising immediately, get out of the heat, and continue drinking fluids.

When the mercury drops...

- Dress in layers (T-shirt and/or long underwear, turtleneck, sweat shirt, and jacket) to maximize your body's warmth. Remember, it's always better to wear several layers of clothing than one heavy layer.

- Wear a hat, since up to 40 percent of your body heat is lost through the neck and head. Then rub a little petroleum jelly on your lips and exposed areas of the skin to prevent chapping.

- Wear mittens, gloves, or wool socks to protect your hands. Mittens keep hands warmer than gloves.

- Drink plenty of water, because water is lost through your nose and mouth when the air is dry.

- "Go out" facing the wind and "come in" with the wind. This helps prevent exposure to windchill when you're wearing sweat-soaked clothing.

- Make fitness a family affair. Build a snowman with your kids or take up a new family hobby such as ice skating or cross-country skiing.

When it's raining...

- Exercise in the "great indoors." Walk in shopping malls, office hall-ways, or indoor tracks, and opt for taking the stairs rather than riding the elevator.

- Invest in home exercise equipment such as a stationary bike, treadmill, or mini-trampoline, so you have alternative activities ready and available. Or turn on an exercise video instead of a sit-com, and exercise along with it.

- Join and use your community fitness center or local YMCA.

45

ACTIVATE YOUR DAY.

Our highly mechanized society seems to encourage everything but exercise. We ride rather than walk, use elevators instead of stairs, push remote controls instead of our bodies. Whatever we have to do, there seems to be a machine to help us do it with little or no effort.

No one is suggesting we go back to the "good old days." However, consider this fact: The number of obese people in this country has greatly increased since 1900, despite a decrease in caloric intake. In other words, we're eating less than our ancestors but gaining more. Why? Partly because we're less active.

Instead of pushing all those buttons to save energy, we need to start pushing our bodies to use energy. Look for ways to use your body more all day long. Any extra activity will help burn excess calories. For example, if you climb stairs rather than ride the elevator for ten minutes a day, in the course of a year, you might burn an additional 66,000 calories or so— that's the equivalent of about 19 pounds of excess body weight (this is an estimate, of course, but you get the point). To activate your daily routine, try some of these "moving" tips:

- Use the stairs instead of the elevator or escalator.
- Park at the far end of the mall parking lot, then walk to the door.
- Get off the bus a stop early and walk the rest of the way.
- Don't drive distances less than ½ mile; walk or ride a bike.
- Walk around while you talk on the phone.
- Walk your dog.
- Deliver messages in person.
- Take a short exercise break instead of a coffee break.
- Ride a stationary bike or stretch while watching television.
- Mow and rake the yard.
- Wash the car yourself.
- Go out dancing instead of sitting at a movie.
- Take a walk instead of lingering over leftovers.

46

MEASURE YOUR PROGRESS MONTHLY.

Changes on the scale are often meaningless. Even though you may be achieving your eating and exercise goals, the scale does not necessarily respond consistently to the changes you've made or the work you've accomplished.

With exercise, for instance, you might lose more inches than pounds. So, even if the scale showed little or no progress over a few months, you might be getting trimmer by the day (replacing pounds of body fat with pounds of lean tissue). A better and more positive way to measure progress is to record the inches disappearing from your arms, chest, waist, and/or thighs. So, every month, use a measuring tape to measure the circumferences of your targeted zones, and complete the accompanying tracking form.

> ### HINT
>
> Take measurements to the nearest ¼ inch with a cloth measuring tape. It is helpful to select some easily identified body landmarks so that you can measure the same place each time. For example, measure next to a mole on your arm or thigh. Your belly button is a made-to-order landmark for measuring your abdomen.

Be patient, though; even changes in size occur slowly. It will take about four weeks to see a measurable change. In addition to body measurements, you'll want to look for other measures of success such as clothes and jewelry getting looser and notches tightening on your belt.

Chart for Recording Your Measurements					
Body circumference (inches)	Date	Date	Date	Date	Date
Arm					
Chest					
Waist					
Abdomen					
Hips					
Thigh					

47

CHOOSE WHERE TO LOSE— HEALTH CLUB OR HOME.

Now that you know how essential a fitness program can be to your long-term success, you may be considering joining a health club so that you have a place to go when it's time to exercise. That's great, because many clubs offer a wide variety of fitness equipment and classes. And once you join a club, you're sure to start working out, right?

People join health clubs with only the best of intentions. Some of them visit the club a couple of times, maybe take a class or two, then never darken the doors again. If this has ever happened to you, you're not alone. Health clubs plan on members not coming to the club regularly, just as casinos depend on people losing money in the long run.

Consider the following issues before you take the health-club plunge:

Time flies. Going to a health club takes extra time and energy. If you're someone who is very busy, consider whether your money is more wisely spent on a good piece of home fitness equipment. Busy people typically have the easiest time exercising first thing in the morning, before leaving the house and before unexpected meetings, phone calls, or people can conflict with their scheduled workout.

Location, location, location. A health club should be conveniently located so that it does not take a great deal of time to get there from either work or home. If the travel time to and from the club is close to, or exceeds, the length of your workout, consider the benefits of an at-home workout.

Crowd control. Take into account the time of day you plan to use the health club. If you want to exercise after work, keep in mind that 5 P.M. to 7 P.M. is often "prime time" at health clubs. If the club is too crowded, you might not get to use the piece of equipment you wanted to. Visit the club during the times you plan to be there to check out the scene. Be aware of any time limitations on aerobic equipment during peak hours. Listen to the music playing and look the crowd over to see whether or not this is a scene that you'll want to visit regularly.

Beautiful bodies. Health clubs can be havens for "perfect 10's." Consider your personal feelings about exercising in public before joining a club. Some people are embarrassed by their bodies and feel self-conscious wearing workout clothing in front of others, particularly members of the opposite sex. For others, the health club is a great place to meet people who have a common interest.

Fitness goals. Some fitness goals are easier to achieve from your home than others are. If you intend to concentrate on losing weight through aerobic fitness, there are many at-home options available. However, if you are motivated by the companionship of others, an aerobics class at a club might be "just what the doctor ordered."

If you have your heart set on becoming a statuesque body builder, the initial investment in equipment for an at-home program would be high. Many health clubs have personal trainers who can help you design a workout to meet your goals and help you feel comfortable using all of the equipment safely. If this is your choice, be sure to check the credentials of either an aerobics instructor or a personal trainer for certification by a recognized national organization.

48

KEEP LEARNING THROUGH HEALTHY HOTLINES.

In this book, we've given you the tools and strategies you need to evaluate your current habits and lifestyle and make healthy changes that can help you lose weight and keep it off. It will take some effort on your part, however. And you may find that as you proceed, you have additional questions about nutrition, foods, and exercise—questions that are beyond the scope of this book. You may wonder how your weight-loss efforts will affect your diabetes or your blood-cholesterol levels. Or you may have questions about a nutrition-related news item that you've read or about some diet aid that you've seen advertised.

Unfortunately, thousands of dieters are seduced daily by promises that pills, potions, or miracle foods will take off and keep off unwanted pounds. These and other diet-related frauds are a multimillion-dollar industry, and if you fall prey to it, it can cost you money, time, even your health. What's more, with so much information out there—some of it contradictory—it can be tough to make heads or tails of what's best for you.

Many people assume that they are protected from misleading weight-loss information; that it can't be published in a book or magazine unless it's true. For example, if a weight-loss book is written by someone with a Ph.D., it is often accepted by unwary consumers as dietary gospel. The sad truth is that anyone can hold a Ph.D. from a diploma mill after taking unaccredited correspondence-school courses of little scientific validity. In fact, one leading medical expert obtained a nutrition diploma for his pet cat by sending $50 to an unaccredited school.

So what can you do? There are many reputable resources that can help you sort out the facts. Your personal health-care provider is a valuable resource who can provide you with helpful information and referrals. And additional help may be just a phone call away. Just call one of the health hotlines listed below. Some of the hotlines are even staffed by registered dietitians.

Consumer Nutrition Hotline of the American Diatetic Association
800-366-1655
Offers nutrition advice from registered dietitians.

The American Institute for Cancer Research Nutrition Hotline
800-843-8114
Offers nutrition advice from registered dietitians.

National Health Information Center
800-336-4797

American Diabetes Association
800-232-3472

American Heart Association
800-AHA-USA1 (242-8721)

National Eating Disorders Organization
918-481-4044

Overeaters Anonymous
505-891-2664

49

STOP A SETBACK FROM BECOMING A RELAPSE.

Think about taking up a new hobby or sport—skiing, for instance. Imagine yourself getting off the lift at the top of the hill for the first time. You look down at the steep ice- and snow-covered slope. You push off and glide gracefully and effortlessly down the hill. Sound like a fantasy? It is! Yet this is how many people approach the "sport" of weight control. Just as it's unlikely that sheer determination and willpower could prevent you from a tumble your first time down an icy hill, it's unlikely that sheer willpower will prevent you from having "tumbles" as you learn to control your weight. Becoming an excellent skier requires a great deal of skill—acquired only through much practice. Similarly, weight control takes skillpower, not willpower.

The most important weight-control skill a "novice" can learn is how to quickly recover from a "fall." We call these "falls" setbacks. A setback can be big or small. It can be a day's exercise missed, a week of diary keeping skipped, or a 20-pound weight gain. Setbacks are hazardous not because of the isolated event itself but because of the way we typically react to it. People who successfully control their weight quickly learn to control their self-talk and attitude toward setbacks. They learn skills to prevent a "slip" from becoming an avalanche.

What Works	**What Hurts**
Expecting and planning for temporary setbacks	Expecting perfection. "All or nothing" thinking. "If I can't be perfect, there's no sense in following my plan."
Confronting the setback as soon as possible and taking some immediate action, like recording it in your diary.	Denial. Pretending the setback did not occur. "I'm just celebrating this special occasion; it'll never happen again."

What Works

Making positive, affirming statements about your past successes. Stating positive action you can take.

Putting the setback into perspective. Acknowledging the deviation from your weight-control plan and comparing it against the progress you've already made.

Taking each setback seriously without exaggerating the situation. Identifying events that contributed to the setback. Adhering to a structured plan. Quickly seeking outside support if necessary to prevent a slip from becoming a relapse.

What Hurts

Punishing or berating yourself through your own negative self-talk. Exaggerating the situation. "I always blow it!" "I'll make myself jog two miles tomorrow."

Seeing the setback as "the first domino to fall." Allowing feelings of guilt and hopelessness to enter your mind. "I'm a hopeless failure."

Making excuses and rationalizations. Minimizing the setback and failing to take action immediately. "I only regained five pounds. That's nothing!"

50

CREATE A LIFELONG PLAN OF ACTION.

The news these days seems filled with prophecies of doom and gloom when it comes to keeping weight off. Is this really an impossible challenge? The answer from the pros at Duke University's Diet & Fitness Center is absolutely...NOT! In fact, research is ongoing at Duke to determine how successful losers remain slim and trim even five years after their weight loss.

DUKE'S TOP TEN WEIGHT-MAINTENANCE STRATEGIES

1. **Live an active life.** No doubt about it—exercise is your number one defense against gaining weight. Numerous studies have shown that exercise is the best predictor of long-term weight maintenance.

2. **Keep a diary.** The first step in making behavioral change is awareness. Diary keeping helps you become aware of your patterns and encourages you to plan your meals and exercise.

3. **Practice skillpower, not willpower**. Being proficient at weight maintenance takes practice and experience, not willpower.

4. **Focus on the journey, not the destination.** Success is not an endpoint that happens when your goal weight is reached. Instead, it's an ongoing process, reinforced each time you make a lifestyle change. Never put your life on hold waiting to reach a certain weight.

5. **Make your lifestyle plan work for you.** Only make changes that you can adapt well to the way you want to live. If you hate to cook, planning your diet around gourmet, home-cooked meals is probably unrealistic.

6. **Look within.** Motivation that comes from within rather than from the outside works best. Changing habits because you believe you deserve a healthy, fit body will keep your motivation strong. Changing to please your doctor, partner, or parent is likely to be motivation that quickly dwindles.

7. **Make changes gradually.** Think evolution, not revolution. Gradual changes feel more natural and are more easily adjusted to and maintained. Congratulate yourself for each and every "baby step."

8. **Surround yourself with support.** Spend time with those individuals who will be consistently supportive of your goals; those individuals may include friends, family, or members of a support group.

9. **Seek to improve your quality of life.** Notice how each small change in habits leads to a corresponding improvement in your enjoyment of life.

10. **Remain ever vigilant.** Always be aware of high-risk situations and events in your life. Take action whenever you feel yourself slipping into old habits.

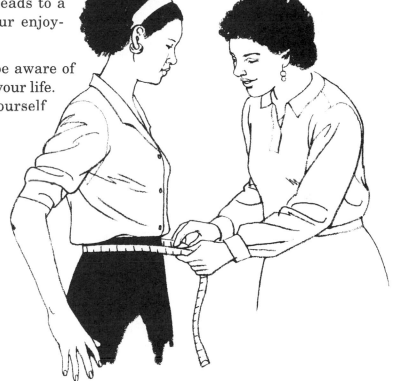

Date_____   Daily Record

MEAL PLAN

	FOOD	PORTION	CALORIES	FAT (G)
BREAKFAST				

Total Calories_____

	FOOD	PORTION	CALORIES	FAT (G)
LUNCH				

Total Calories_____

	FOOD	PORTION	CALORIES	FAT (G)
DINNER				

Total Calories_____

PLANNED EATING   Total Calories_____

UNPLANNED EATING

TIME	FOOD	CALORIES	SITUATION/FEELINGS

Total Daily Calories_____
(Include any calories from unplanned eating)

Date_____			Daily Record

MEAL PLAN

	FOOD	**PORTION**	**CALORIES**	**FAT (G)**
BREAKFAST				
			Total Calories_____	
LUNCH				
			Total Calories_____	
DINNER				
			Total Calories_____	

PLANNED EATING   Total Calories_____

UNPLANNED EATING

TIME	**FOOD**	**CALORIES**	**SITUATION/FEELINGS**

Total Daily Calories_____
(Include any calories from unplanned eating)

EXERCISE PLAN

ACTIVITY	DURATION	COMMENTS
Aerobic:		
Strength:		
Stretching:		

THINKING ABOUT TODAY

How I felt about myself today:

What I did well today:

How I can make tomorrow better:

"A goal without a plan is just a *wish*"